hampsteadtheatre

The Nuffield southampton

hampsteadtheatre
and The Nuffield Theatre, Southampton present

the president's holiday

by Penny Gold

pp 89-90-91

Production Sponsor

pembertons property management

A&B
Arts & Business *working together*

Corporate Partner of **hampstead**theatre's Russian Plays. Plays include
The President's Holiday, *Three Sisters on Hope Street* and *War and Peace*.
❖ SALANS

hampsteadtheatre gratefully acknowledges
the support of

Funded by Camden Council

hampsteadtheatre and The Nuffield Theatre, Southampton present

the president's holiday

by **Penny Gold**

Cast

Raisa Gorbachev	**Isla Blair**
Yuri Plekhanov	**Robert Demeger**
Mikhail Gorbachev	**Julian Glover**
Irina	**Anna Hewson**
Anatoly	**Roger May**
Kseniya	**Amy Jane Cotter**
	Ella O'Brien
Nastenka	**Sophie Cornelius**
	Skye Stuart

Creative Team

Director	**Patrick Sandford**
Set and Costume Designer	**Robin Don**
Lighting Designer	**David W. Kidd**
Sound Designer	**Marcus Christensen**
Video Designer	**Sophie Phillips**
Associate Lighting Designer	**Peter Gibson**
Costume Supervisor	**Hilary Lewis**
Casting Director	**Siobhan Bracke**
Channel 4 Resident Director	**Noah Birksted-Breen**
Company Stage Manager	**Kristi Warwick**
Deputy Stage Manager	**Helen Smith**
Assistant Stage Manager	**Martha Mamo**
Chaperone	**Lauren Glassman**
heat&**light** Supervisor	**Debra Glazer**
Wardrobe Maintenance	**Greg Dunn**
Make-up Artist	**David Stoneman**
Set Built by	**TMS International Ltd**
Press Representative	**Becky Sayer** (020 7449 4151)

hampsteadtheatre would like to thank:
Open Air Theatre – Regents Park, Simon Slater

The President's Holiday **was first performed at Hampstead Theatre, London,
on Thursday 17 January 2008**

cast and creative team

Penny Gold (Writer)
Stage plays include: *When We Are Rich* (Nuffield Theatre, Southampton); *Burning in Heaven* (Old Red Lion); *Riptide* (Weaver Hughes Ensemble, Jerwood Centre); *Lazarus and Others* (Freehand Theatre Co.); *I Was Shakespeare's Double* (with John Downie, RSC, The Other Place). For BBC Radio, plays include: *In the Keep Net*, *Dear Brother...*, *Old Man Goya*, *Three Days that Shook the World*, serial dramatisation of Margaret Forster's novel *Shadow Baby*, adaptations of Wole Soyinka's *Death and the King's Horseman* and Howard Brenton's *Bloody Poetry*. Penny began her career working for the director John Barton at the RSC. Since then she has been an editor and producer for BBC Television and Film and a commissioning editor/producer/director for BBC Radio Drama for whom she still directs as an Independent. She has also been a theatre literary manager and continues to do dramaturgical work for several companies.

Isla Blair (*Raisa Gorbachev*)
Recent theatre includes: *The History Boys* (National Theatre/ Wyndhams); *Mrs Pat* (York Theatre Royal); *Stuff Happens*, *A Funny Thing Happened on the Way to the Forum*, *Noises Off* (National Theatre); *Waters of the Moon* (Salisbury Playhouse); *Mrs Warren's Profession* (Bristol Old Vic); *Six Degrees of Separation* (Sheffield Crucible); *One Flew Over the Cuckoo's Nest* (Centreline Productions); *Tartuffe* (PW Prods). Regional theatre includes: *Kiss Me Kate*, *Hobson's Choice*, *Black Comedy*, *Othello*, *The Browning Version*, *Abelard and Heloise*, *The Cherry Orchard*, *Vivat Regina*, *Jumpers* (Bristol Old Vic); *Private Lives*, *A Doll's House* (Yvonne Arnauld, Guilford/tours); *The Paldock*, *Miss in her Teens*, *King Lear*, *Twelfth Night*, *What the Butler Saw*, *Miss Julie*, *The Rivals*, *Boswell's Life of Johnson* (Prospect Theatre Company). Recent television includes: *Casualty*, *Quatermass Experiment*, *Midsomer Murders*, *House of Cards – The Final Cut*, *Holby City*, *Dalziel and Pascoe*, *A Touch of Frost*, *Inspector Morse*, *The Advocates*, *Heartbeat*, *Heaven on Earth*. Recent films include: *Afterlife*, *Mrs Caldicot's Cabbage War*, *The Match*. Earlier films include: *Treasure Island*, *Indiana Jones and the Last Crusade*.

Robert Demeger (*Yuri Plekhanov*)
Theatre includes: *Romeo and Juliet*, *King John*, *Henry VI*, *As You Like It*, *Macbeth*, *The Balcony* (RSC); *The Winter's Tale*, *Coriolanus* (English Shakespeare Company/world tour/Aldwych); *Marya* (Old Vic); *Medea*, *The Duchess of Malfi* (Wyndhams); *The Rules of the Game*, *The Doctor's Dilemma*, *The Jew of Malta* (Almeida); *Trelawney of the Wells*, *The Seagull* (National Theatre); *A Busy Day* (Lyric); *Oxygen* (Riverside Studios); Pirandello's *Henry IV* (Donmar); *The Taming of the Shrew*, *Hamlet* (Thelma Holt/national tours); *Julius Caesar* (Barbican/Paris/ Madrid/Luxembourg); *The Woman in Black* (Fortune Theatre/national tour). Regional theatre includes: *Twelfth Night*, *The Elephant Man* (Contact Theatre, Manchester); *Who's Afraid of Virginia Woolf?* (Wolsey Theatre, Ipswich); *A Christmas Carol*, *The Merchant of Venice* (Palace

Theatre, Westcliff); *The Tempest, Measure for Measure* (Deborah Warner's Kick Theatre); *King Lear* (Kick Theatre/Almeida/Egypt/ Yugoslavia); Michael Grandage's productions of *Edward II* and *Richard III* (Sheffield Crucible); *Vieux Carré* (Library Theatre, Manchester); *The Glass Cage* (Theatre Royal Northampton). Recent television includes: *Waking the Dead, Doctor Who, He Kills Coppers.* Film includes: *Little Dorrit, Wuthering Heights, Different for Girls, The Young Poisoner's Handbook, Orlando, Secret Passage, Longitude.*

Julian Glover (*Mikhail Gorbachev*)
Theatre credits include: John Betjeman in *All Our Hellos and Goodbyes* (St. Pancras Station); *The Voysey Inheritance, Chips with Everything, Jumpers* (National Theatre); *The Soldier's Tale, Richard II, Prayers of Sherkin, Hamlet* (Old Vic); *King Lear, Anthony and Cleopatra* (Shakespeare's Globe); *A Penny for a Song* (Whitehall Theatre); *The Dresser* (Duke of York's Theatre); *Phèdre/Britannicus* (Almeida at The Albery); *Waiting for Godot* (Piccadilly Theatre); *An Inspector Calls* (National Theatre/Aldwych); *Cyrano de Bergerac* (Haymarket Theatre); *Never the Sinner* (Playhouse Theatre); *Coriolanus, Henry VI Parts 1, 2 & 3, The Man of Mode, Subject to Fits, Cousin Vladimir, The Changeling* (RSC); *Beowulf* (Lyric Hammersmith and World Tour); *Otherwise Engaged* (Queens Theatre); *The Constant Couple* (Wyndhams Theatre); *The Knack, Naked, Luther, Altona* (Royal Court). Recent regional theatre includes: *The Tempest* (Nuffield Theatre); *Shadowlands* (Salisbury Playhouse); *Man and Superman, Galileo's Daughter* (Peter Hall Company, Theatre Royal Bath); *Taking Sides* (The Touring Consortium); *Macbeth* (Albery Theatre); *Hamlet* (Norwich Playhouse); *In Praise of Love* (Theatre Royal Bath/tour); *Julius Caesar, Romeo and Juliet, Henry IV Parts 1 & 2* (RSC); *All My Sons* (Palace Theatre, Watford); *The Aspern Papers* (Redgrave Theatre). Recent television credits include: *Silent Witness, Trial and Retribution, Waking the Dead, The Fight Master, Midsomer Murders, Brother Cadfael, Taggart.* Recent film credits include: *Young Victoria, Mirrors, Troy, Two Men Went To War, Harry Potter and the Chamber Of Secrets.* Other films include: *For Your Eyes Only, The Empire Strikes Back, Indiana Jones and the Last Crusade, The Young Victoria,* and the legendary *Tom Jones.*

Anna Hewson (*Irina*)
Theatre includes: *The Canterbury Tales* (RSC/West End/tour); *Play and Not I* (Battersea Arts Centre); *Map of the Heart* (Salisbury Playhouse); *The Importance of Being Earnest, The Happiest Days of Your Life* (Royal Exchange, Manchester); *Triumph of Love* (Watermill Theatre); *Women of Troy, The Caucasian Chalk Circle, Have You Anything to Declare?, The Three Sisters* (Orange Tree Theatre); Television includes: *Holby City.*

Roger May (*Anatoly*)
Theatre includes: *The Last Confession* (Chichester and Theatre Royal Haymarket); *Troilus and Cressida* (Edinburgh International Festival/RSC); *Private Lives* (Basingstoke); *Hamlet* (Cannizaro Park, Wimbledon); *Twelfth Night, And a Nightingale Sang, Much Ado About Nothing* (Nuffield Theatre, Southampton); *Richard III, Julius Caesar* (RSC); *Time*

and Time Again (national tour); *All's Well That Ends Well* (ACTER); *The Mayor of Casterbridge*, *What the Butler Saw* (Exeter); *The Jail Diary of Albie Sachs* (Canadian Tour). Television includes: *Britz, White King Red Rubber Black Death*, *The Cazalet Chronicles, Close and True, Just Desserts, Starting Out, Peak Practice, Every Woman Knows a Secret, Hornblower, Mosley, Jeremiah*. Film includes: *The Scarlet Tunic, The Titchborne Claimant, Out of Darkness, An Ideal Husband*. Roger has recorded over 100 plays, short stories and readings for radio and has twice been a member of the BBC Radio Drama Company. He plays James Bellamy in *The Archers*. He has also recorded a number of books including: *The Day of the Triffids, Death on the Nile, War of the Worlds*.

Sophie Cornelius, Amy Jane Cotter, Ella O'Brien and **Skye Stuart** are all members of the **heat&light** company – **hampstead**theatre's youth theatre.

Patrick Sandford (Director)
Patrick is Artistic Director of The Nuffield Theatre, Southampton. New plays include: *The Winter Wife* by Claire Tomalin, also at the Lyric Theatre Hammersmith (Best Director, TMA awards); *Exchange* by Yuri Trifonov, adapted by Michael Frayn (transferred to the Vaudeville Theatre); *In Broad Daylight* by Lesley Bruce, also at the Tricycle Theatre, Kilburn; *The Dramatic Attitiudes of Miss Fanny Kemble* by Claire Luckham; *The Shagaround* by Maggie Nevill, also at Soho Theatre; *When We Are Rich* by Penny Gold. British premieres of foreign plays include: Woody Allen's *The Floating Lightbulb*; *Dead White Males* by David Williamson; *The John Wayne Principle* by Tony MacNamara, also at The Pleasance, London. Classics include: *Twelfth Night*, also in French at the Théâtre des 2 Rives, Rouen, France; Euripides' *The Bacchae*, Sophocles' *Oedipus Rex,* also at the ancient amphitheatre in Paphos, Cyprus, *Hamlet*, Schiller's *Mary Stuart*, and Chekhov's *Three Sisters* (nominated for Best Touring Production, TMA Awards). Abroad, his productions have been seen in Australia, France, Germany, South Africa and recently Barbados. Translation work includes: *Beach Wedding* by Didier Van Cauwelaert. Patrick was previously Artistic Director of the Lyric Theatre, Belfast, producing new work by Stewart Parker, Graham Reid and Christina Reid.

Robin Don (Set and Costume Designer)
Theatre credits include: *The Emperor Jones, The Ticket-of-Leave Man* (National Theatre); *Twelfth Night, Les Enfants du Paradis* (RSC); *Kiss of the Spider Woman, The Marshalling Yard, When I Was A Girl I Used to Scream and Shout* (Bush Theatre); *Beautiful Thing* (Bush Theatre/ Duke of York's); *Someone Who'll Watch Over Me* (Hampstead Theatre/ Booth Theatre, Broadway); *A Walk in the Woods* (Comedy Theatre); *Hotel Paradiso* (National Theatre Iceland); *Frankenstein, Hamlet, Salomé* (Nuffield Theatre, Southampton); *Fool for Love* (Donmar Warehouse); *The Anniversary* (Liverpool Playhouse and Garrick); *The Winter Guest, The Storm* (Almeida Theatre); *Three Sisters* (Playhouse); *Bent* (New Ambassadors Theatre); plus numerous designs for Opera House worldwide.

David W. Kidd (Lighting Designer)
Most recent work includes: *Peter and the Wolf* (Ballet Flanders/Royal Carré Theatre, Amsterdam/UK tour); *Andersen's Fairy Tales* (Bulgarian National Ballet at Opera Sophia); *Die Walküre* (Den Ny Opera, Denmark); *Unsuspecting Susan* (New York); *She Stoops to Conquer, Tchaikovsky and the Queen of Spades* (Nuffield Theatre, Southampton); *Lotte's Journey* (The New End Theatre). West End and London credits include: *The Anniversary, The Female Odd Couple, The Dice House, Mademoiselle Colombe, From the Hart, Paul Merton Live!* at the Palladium plus numerous designs for the National Youth Theatre and leading producing theatres across the UK.

Marcus Christensen (Sound Designer)
Theatre includes as Associate Sound Designer: *Measure for Measure* (RSC); *Waiting for Godot* (New Ambassadors); *Amy's View* (Garrick); *Old Times* (Brighton Theatre Royal/tour/Bath Theatre Royal); *Journey's End* (New Ambassadors); *What the Butler Saw* (Criterion); *The Hound of the Baskervilles* (Mercury Theatre). As Sound Designer: *Life after Scandal* (Hampstead Theatre); *Private Lives, Dangerous Obsession, The Rivals* (Bath Theatre Royal/tour); *The Promise, She Stoops to Conquer, Death of a Salesman, Small Miracle, Miss Julie, Blue Sky State, Devil's Advocate, A Midsummer Night's Dream, Of Mice and Men, The Resistible Rise of Arturo Ui, The Seagull* (Mercury Theatre). As Production Sound Engineer: *The Schuman Plan, What the Butler Saw* (Hampstead Theatre); *Journey's End* (New Ambassadors/tour); *See How They Run* (Duchess Theatre/tour); *Love Songs* (New Ambassadors); *Take Flight* (Menier Chocolate Factory); *...And Then There Were None* (Gielgud); *A Voyage Round My Father, Honour* (Wyndhams); *National Anthems, The Philadelphia Story* (Old Vic).

Sophie Phillips (Video Designer)
Theatre includes: *Puss in Boots* (puppet and prop-maker, Library Theatre, Manchester); *Life After Scandal* (Hampstead Theatre); *Hamlet* (York Theatre Royal, York Prize Winner, Speculative Design Project); *Day Return* (Left Luggage Theatre, Realised Performance, Nottingham); *Bestiary* (design and publicity, Buxton Fringe Festival); *The Visit* (Speculative Design Project, West Yorkshire Playhouse); *The Pillowman* (lighting assistant and puppeteer, ITV Six Play Festival, Nottingham); *Once in a Lifetime* (work placement, painter, National Theatre); *Six Degrees of Separation* (work placement, props, Royal Exchange Theatre, Manchester).

Peter Gibson (Associate Lighting Designer)
Theatre credits for the Nuffield Theatre, Southampton include: *Two Beats to the Bar, Animal Farm, Waiting for Godot, A Taste of Honey, The Caretaker, Look Back in Anger, Bolt Hole, Two, Three in a Bed, The Brothers of the Brush*. As a freelance electrician credits include: *Cabaret* (Lyric); *Cats* (tour); *Blood Brothers* (tour); *Joseph* (New London/tour); *Whistle Down the Wind, Lazy Town, Sing-A-Long-A-Abba, Doctor Dolittle, Rough Music, Treasure Island*.

hampsteadtheatre is one of the UK's leading new-writing venues housed in a magnificent purpose-built state-of-the-art theatre – a company that is fast approaching its fiftieth year of operation.

hampsteadtheatre has a mission: to find, develop, and produce new plays to the highest possible standards, for as many people as we can encourage to see them. Its work is both national and international in its scope and ambition.

hampsteadtheatre exists to take risks and to discover the talent of the future. New writing is our passion. We consistently create the best conditions for writers to flourish and are rewarded with diverse award-winning and far-reaching plays.

The list of playwrights who had their early work produced at **hampstead**theatre who are now filling theatres all over the country and beyond include Mike Leigh, Michael Frayn, Brian Friel, Terry Johnson, Hanif Kureishi, Simon Block, Abi Morgan, Rona Munro, Tamsin Oglesby, Harold Pinter, Philip Ridley, Shelagh Stephenson, debbie tucker green, Crispin Whittell and Roy Williams. The careers of actors Jude Law, Alison Steadman, Jane Horrocks and Rufus Sewell were launched at **hampstead**theatre.

Each year the theatre invites the most exciting writers around to write for us. At least half of these playwrights will be emerging writers who are just hitting their stride – writers who we believe are on the brink of establishing themselves as important new voices. We also ask mid-career and mature playwrights to write for us on topics they are burning to explore.

hampsteadtheatre's role as one of the finest new writing venues in London is made possible by the generous support of our Luminary members. We would like to thank the following individuals and companies for ensuring the future of our artistic and educational programmes.

our current luminaries are:

(as of November 2007)

thank you to the following for supporting our creativity:

Abbey Charitable Trust; Acacia Charitable Trust; The Andor Charitable Trust; Anglo American; Arimathea Charitable Trust; Arts & Business; Awards for All; Auerbach Trust Charity; Bank Leumi; BBC Children in Need; The Basil Samuels Charitable Trust; Bennetts Associates; Big Lottery Fund; Blick Rothenberg; Bridge House Estates Trust Fund; The Chapman Charitable Trust; Swiss Cottage Area Partnership; Community Fund; The John S Cohen Foundation; Coutts Charitable Trust; D'Oyly Carte Charitable Trust; The Dorset Foundation; Duis Charitable Trust; The Eranda Foundation; The Ernest Cook Trust; European Association of Jewish Culture; Garrick Charitable Trust; Gerald Ronson Foundation; The Hampstead & Highgate Express; Hampstead, Wells & Campden Trust; Help a London Child; Harold Hyam Wingate Foundation; The Jack Petchey Foundation; Jacobs Charitable Trust; John Lyon's Charity Trust; Kennedy Leigh Charitable Trust; Local Network Fund; Mackintosh Foundation; Markson Pianos; Marriot Hotel, Regents Park; Milly Apthorp Charitable Trust; The Morel Trust: The Noël Coward Foundation; Notes Productions Ltd; Parkheath Estates: The Paul Hamlyn Foundation: Pembertons Property Management; The Rayne Foundation; Reed Elsevier; Richard Reeves Foundation; Royal Victoria Hall Foundation; Salans; Samuel French; The Shoresh Foundation; Society for Theatre Research; Solomon Taylor Shaw: Sweet and Maxwell; Karl Sydow; Towry Law; The Vandervell Foundation; The Vintners' Company; World Jewish Relief; Charles Wolfson Foundation; Zurich Community Trust.

 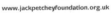

If you would like to become more closely involved, and would like to help us find the talent and the audiences of the future, please call Tamzin Robertson on 020 7449 4171 or email development@hampsteadtheatre.com

capital campaign supporters

hampsteadtheatre would like to thank the following donors who kindly contributed to the Capital Campaign, enabling us to build our fantastic new home.

Mr Robert Adams
Mr Robert Ainscow
Mrs Farah Alaghband
Mr W Aldwinckle
Mr Mark Allison
Anonymous
Mrs Klari Atkin
Mr William Atkins
Mr and Mrs Daniel and Pauline Auerbach
Mr David Aukin
Sir Alan Ayckbourn
Mr George Bailey
Mr Christopher Beard
Mr Eric Beecham
Mrs Lucy Ben-Levi
Mr Alan Bennett
Mr and Mrs Rab Bennetts
Mr Roger Berlind
Ms Vicky Biles
Mr Michael Blakemore
Mr Simon Block
Mr A Bloomfield
Mr John Bolton
Mr Peter Borender
Mr and Mrs Rob and Colleen Brand
Mr Matthew Broadbent
Mr Alan Brodie
Dr John and Dorothy Brook
Mr Leonard Bull
Mr and Mrs Paul and Ossie Burger
Ms Kathy Burke
Mr O Burstin
Ms Deborah Buzan
Mr Charles Caplin
Sir Trevor and Susan Chinn
Mr Martin Cliff
Mr Michael Codron
Mr and Mrs Denis Cohen
Dr David Cohen
Mr David Cornwell
Mr and Mrs Sidney and Elizabeth Corob
Mr and Mrs John Crosfield
Miss Nicci Crowther
Ms Hilary Dane
Mr and Mrs Ralph Davidson
Mr and Mrs Gerald Davidson
Mrs Deborah Davis
Mr Edwin Davison
Mr David Day
Ms Frankie de Freitas
Mr and Mrs David and Jose Dent

Professor Christopher and Elizabeth Dickinson
Sir Harry Djanogly
Ms Lindsay Duncan
Mr David Dutton
Mrs Myrtle Ellenbogen
Mr Michael Elwyn
Mr Tom Erhardt
Sir Richard Eyre
Mr Peter Falk
Ms Nina Finburgh
Mr and Mrs George and Rosamund Fokschaner
Ms Lisa Forrell
Mr N Forsyth
Mr Freddie Fox
Mr Michael Frayn
Mr Norman Freed
Mr Conrad Freedman
Mr and Mrs Robert and Elizabeth Freeman
Mr and Mrs Jeremy and Susan Freeman
Mr and Mrs Brian Friel
Mr Arnold Fulton
Mr and Mrs Michael and Jacqueline Gee
Mr and Mrs Jonathan and Jacqueline Gestetner
Mr Desmond Goch
Mr Anthony Goldstein
Mr Andrew Goodman
Ms Niki Gorick
Mrs Katerina Gould
Lord and Lady Grabiner
Mr and Mrs Jonathan Green
Mr and Mrs David Green
Mrs Susan Green
Mr Nicholas Greenstone
Mr Michael Gross
Mr and Mrs Paul Hackworth
Dr Peter and Elaine Hallgarten
Miss Susan Hampshire
Mr Christopher Hampton
Mr Laurence Harbottle
Sir David Hare
Lady Pamela Harlech
Mr Paul Harris
Mr John Harrison
Mr Howard Harrison
Mr Jonathan Harvey
Sir Maurice Hatter
Mr Marc Hauer
Dr Samuel Hauer
Mr and Mrs Michael and Morven Heller

Mr Philip Hobbs
Mr and Mrs Robin and Inge Hyman
Mr Nicholas Hytner
Ms Phoebe Isaacs
Mr Michael Israel
Professor Howard and Sandra Jacobs
Mr and Mrs Max Jacobs
Dr C Kaplanis
Mrs Patricia Karet
Baroness Helena Kennedy
Mrs Ann Kieran
Mr Jeremy King
Mr Peter Knight
Sir Eddie Kulukundis
Ms Belinda Lang
Mr and Mrs Edward Lee
Mrs Janette Lesser
Lady Diane Lever
Mr Daniel Levy
Mr Peter Levy
Sir Sydney and Lady Lipworth
Mrs Alyssa Lovegrove
Ms Sue MacGregor
Mr S Magee
Mr Fouad Malouf
Mr and Mrs Lee Manning
Mr and Mrs Thomas and Karen Mautner
Mr and Mrs David and Sandra Max
Mrs June McCall
Mr John McFadden
Mr Ewan McGregor
Mr and Mrs David Meller
Mr Raymond Mellor
Mr Anthony Minghella
Mr and Mrs David Mirvish
Mr and Mrs Mark Mishon
Mr and Mrs Edward and Diana Mocatta
Mr and Mrs Gary Monnickendam
Mrs and Mrs David and Sandra Montague
Mr Peter Morris
Mr and Mrs Ian Morrison
Mr Andrew Morton
Lady Sara Morton
Mr Gabriel Moss QC
Mr and Mrs Terence Mugliston
Mr and Mrs Roger and Bridget Myddelton
Mr Stewart Nash
Mr James Nederlander

Mr John Newbigin
Sir Trevor Nunn
Mr T Owen
Mr and Mrs Simon and Midge Palley
Mr Barrie Pearson
Mr Daniel Peltz
The Honorable Elizabeth Peltz
Mr Richard Peskin
Mr Gary Phillips
Mr Trevor Phillips
Mrs Gillian Phillips
Mr and Mrs Peter and Wendy Phillips
Mr Paul Phillips
Mr Tim Pigott-Smith
Mr Alan Plater
Mr Michael Platt
Mr and Mrs Brian and Hilary Pomeroy
Mr and Mrs Michael and Tamara Rabin
Mr D Randall
Mrs Janet Rapp
Mr and Mrs Paul and Claire Rayden
Mr Robert Reilly
Mr Dominic Ricketts
Mr Gillespie Robertson
Mr and Mrs Edward Roche
Mr D Rogers
Mr Gerald Ronson and Dame Gail Ronson DBE
Mr Benjamin Rose
Mr and Mrs Anthony and Sue Rosner
Mr Vernon Rosoux
Mrs Patricia Rothman
Mr Robert Rubin
Mr Michael Rudman
Mrs Esther Rudolf
Mrs Coral Samuel
Mr and Mrs Marcus and Andrea Sarner
Sir David and Lady Scholey
Mr James Barrington Serjent
Ms Louisa Service
Mr Cyril Shack
Mr and Mrs Peter Shalson
Mr and Mrs Gerry and Sue Sharp
Mr and Mrs Mike Sherwood
Mr Richard Shuttleworth
Mr and Mrs Jonathan and Lucy Silver
Mr and Mrs Anthony and Beverley Silverstone
Mr and Mrs Michael Simmons
Mr and Mrs Mark Simpson

Mr and Mrs Michael and Zsuzsi Slowe
Mr and Mrs Jeremy Smouha
Mr David Soskin
Dr Michael Spiro
Mr Nicholas Springer
Mr and Mrs Peter Sprinz
Mr Simon Stapely
Miss Imelda Staunton
Mr Bruce Steinberg and Ashley Dartnell
Ms Shelagh Stephenson
Mr Jonathan Stone
Sir Tom Stoppard
Mr David Tabatznik
Mr Paul Taiano
Mrs Valentine Thomas
Mr and Mrs Simon Tindall
Mr Fred Topliffe
Ms Jenny Topper
Mr and Mrs Barry Townsley
Mr Christopher Wade
Mr Vincent Wang
Mr Tom Webster
Mr Timothy West
Mrs L Westbury
Dr Adrian Whiteson
Mrs Judy Williams
Mr James Williams
Mr Richard Wilson
Mr Geoffrey Wilson
Mr Peter Wolff
Lady Ruth Wolfson
Mr and Mrs Fred and Della Worms
Mrs Marion Yass
Mr and Mrs Jeffrey and Fenella Young
Allied Irish Bank
Buro Four Project Services
Casarotto Ramsay and Associates
Charles Caplin & Co
Conway van Gelder Ltd
Ernest R Shaw Insurance Brokers
Friends of Theatre
Garfield Weston Foundation
Ham & Highgate Express
Hampstead Hill School
Hampstead Wells & Campden Trust
J Leon & Company Ltd
John Lyon's Charity
Kleinwort Benson Charitable Trust
Mercers' Company Charitable Trust
N M Rothschild & Sons Ltd

Nyman Libson Paul
Peters Fraser & Dunlop
RAC Plc
Richard Grand Foundation
Samuel French Ltd
The Acacia Charitable Trust
The Agency
The Allen Foundation for the Arts
The Andor Charitable Trust
The Archie Sherman Charitable Trust
The Arthur Andersen Foundation
The Barnett & Sylvia Shine No 2 Charitable Trust
The British Land Company PLC
The Coutts Charitable Trust
The Dent Charitable Trust
The Dorset Foundation
The Drue Heinz Trust
The Duveen Trust
The Equity Trust Fund
The Esmee Fairbairn Foundation
The Follett Trust
The Garrick Charitable Trust
The Harold Hyam Wingate Foundation
The Hollick Family Trust
The John S Cohen Foundation
The Mackintosh Foundation
The Maurice Hatter Foundation
The Monument Trust
The Noel Coward Foundation
The Presidents Club
The Rayne Foundation
The Rose Foundation
The Royal Victoria Hall Foundation
The Sidney & Elizabeth Corob Charitable Trust
The Steel Charitable Trust
The Trusthouse Charitable Foundation
The Ury Trust
The Weinstock Fund
Wild Rose Trust

hampsteadtheatre would also like to thank the many generous donors who we are unable to list individually.

creative learning
widening access to new playwriting

Changing Lives

Our Creative Learning programme is a thriving part of **hampstead**theatre's work. We aim to celebrate all aspects of the creative process in ways which support learning and widen access to the theatre's programme. At its best, our work has the power to change lives.

'My first encounter with Hampstead Theatre was a primary school trip when I was 8 years old. I am now a Peer Ambassador, which involves teaching and assisting drama projects for a range of different age groups. The experience has really boosted my confidence and has made me value responsibility.'
(Youth Theatre Member since 2003)

We work closely with **hampstead**theatre artists and writers to find innovative ways to inspire creativity and develop emerging talent. The programme helps people of all ages to develop personal, social and communication skills. We actively engage with some of the most disadvantaged groups in our local community.

Schools Audiences – Follow Spot

We're offering a limited number of £6 tickets for Excellence In Cities schools in Greater London (available to groups attending midweek matinees and designated performances only). All other schools tickets are £10, with one free ticket for every ten paid.

Our schools audience programme makes a visit to see a show at **hampstead**theatre more meaningful, accessible and educational. Follow Spot offers exciting creative strategies for delivering the curriculum, exploring the creative practice behind a production, and increasing understanding of the creative industries. We provide:

- Free online teacher resources, including complete schemes of work for GCSE and A-Level
- Free play texts (when making a booking)
- Free post-show Q&A with the company and creative team
- Teacher trainings with director or writer (subject to availability, £5 per teacher)
- Bespoke pre- or post-visit workshops

'An inspiration!' 'A real refreshment of skills and ideas.'
'Excellent techniques that I can translate into my own work.'
(Teachers attending training in June 2007)

Call our Schools Tickets Co-ordinator on 020 7722 9301 to book.

Boosting Learning

At the heart of the programme is a network of long-term relationships with teachers and young people at local schools. Through in-school workshops, theatre visits and youth theatre referrals, we help to improve learning, motivation and self esteem. Our script and story-writing projects, for example, offer new, drama-based ways to improve literacy, which in turn boosts learning across all subjects in the curriculum.

'The programme that our school has created in collaboration with Hampstead Theatre and the Royal Court is extensive and is absolutely key to the success of the department, both in terms of exam results and also the wider and less easily evaluated development of students creativity and self worth.'
(Head Of Drama, local secondary school, March 2007)

Act, Write and More with Our Youth Theatre

The **heat&light** Company is made up of budding performers, writers, directors, stage managers and technicians aged 11 to 25. Each term four groups come together to explore the power and potential of theatre in ways which reflect the artistic practice at Hampstead. This year our groups have worked with nine writers, including Jane Bodie, Dennis Kelly and Steve Waters, as well as John Kani and the *Nothing But The Truth* company. **hampstead**theatre's Youth Theatre is free to all participants and produces twelve performances a year.

'The first heat&light term was really good because it felt like there were no rules and you could write, act or do anything you wanted, with the freedom to perform and produce fresh and new ideas. The Daring Pairings project in which I co-wrote and produced a short play with Roy Williams was particularly enjoyable. I am now writing and acting for Channel 4's new show Skins.'
(Youth Theatre Member since 2003)

Creative Learning by Numbers

In the year April 06 – March 07 our outcomes included:

- 11,000 participants, of which 58% from a BME background, at 595 events
- 75 complete projects delivered at the theatre and out in school and community settings
- 83 educational performances in the Michael Frayn Space

If you would like to find out more please email
creativelearning@hampsteadtheatre.com

for **hampstead**theatre

WILL YOU?

Have you ever thought you could support
hampsteadtheatre by leaving a legacy?

hampsteadtheatre is a registered charity that exists
to present new writing for the stage. After years of
outstanding work, the theatre now has a home
to match its reputation for producing some of the most
exhilarating theatre in London.

In addition to producing ten full-scale productions
a year, we:

- Encourage diverse audiences to have a deeper
  understanding and appreciation of new plays in the
  theatre
- Support a successful integrated education
  programme that gives people, and young people in
  particular, the opportunity to participate in a wide
  range of writing and performance projects
- Read and respond to 1800 unsolicited scripts a year

hampsteadtheatre plays and will continue to play a
crucial role in the cultural life of its community.

If you leave a legacy to **hampstead**theatre this is free from tax.

For more information on leaving a legacy to
hampsteadtheatre, please get in touch with the Sarah Coop on
020 7449 4161 or email **sarahc@hampsteadtheatre.com**

The Nuffield
southampton

The Nuffield Theatre situated on the University of Southampton's campus is one of the South's leading producing theatres. Originally opened by the University of Southampton in 1964, The Nuffield Theatre became an independent charitable trust in 1982, funded by Arts Council England, Southampton City Council, Hampshire County Council and the University of Southampton.

Over the last forty years The Nuffield has come to be recognised in England and abroad as a major force in British Theatre. Today, The Nuffield led by its Artistic Director, Patrick Sandford, creates award-winning productions that tour nationally and sometimes internationally.

The theatre also plays host to the world's best national and international touring companies and regularly attracts some of the country's most gifted and well-regarded actors. Visiting shows last season included Peter Brook's *Fragments* by Samuel Becket, *Faustus* from Headlong Theatre and the visually ravishing dance theatre Derevo from St Petersberg amongst others.

The Nuffield has become a vital artistic resource for Southampton and the surrounding area, and invests in developing new artists and productions and provides a full and varied educational and participatory programme. The Nuffield also runs a highly acclaimed writers' group for aspiring playwrights and is home to Hampshire Youth Theatre.

Earlier in 2007 the Company won a tender to run a programme of theatre, dance, music, cabaret and comedy in two theatres in a new arts complex due to open in 2012 in the Guildhall Square in Southampton. This marks a significant expansion for the Company which will also continue to operate its existing theatre as a producing house.

For more information on what's happening at The Nuffield this season please contact the box office on 023 8067 1771 or log onto the website www.nuffieldtheatre.co.uk

THE PRESIDENT'S HOLIDAY

Penny Gold

For my mother

In the 1990s, Reaganites claimed they had 'won' the Cold War and Dr Francis Fukuyama declared 'the end of History'. At the time of writing, the American 'neo-cons' continue to assert that with their economic and military might, the triumph of global capitalism is inevitable. Socialism, they say, is dead. Well, we'll see.

Penny Gold

Characters

MIKHAIL SERGEYEVICH GORBACHEV (Misha), *60,*
    President of USSR
RAISA MAXIMOVNA (Raya), *59, his wife*
IRINA, *34, their daughter*
ANATOLY (Tolya), *35, Irina's husband*
KSENIYA, *12, their daughter*
ANASTASIA (NASTENKA), *9, their daughter*
YURI SERGEYEVICH PLEKHANOV, *61, KGB Head of*
    Security for the President

The play includes pre-recorded radio news bulletins and brief
'Echo' sequences featuring:
GUARD, *to be voiced by actor playing Plekhanov*
CZAR NICHOLAS II, *to be voiced by actor playing Gorbachev*
CZARINA ALEXANDRA, *to be voiced by actress playing*
    Raisa
OLGA, *their eldest daughter, to be voiced by actress playing*
    Irina
ANASTASIA, *youngest daughter, to be voiced by actress*
    playing Kseniya
ALEXIS, *their son, to be voiced by actress playing Nastenka*

Speech in [square brackets] indicates an unspoken or unfinished
thought or statement.

The action takes place between 18th and 21st August 1991 in
the Presidential dacha in Foros, on the Black Sea.

This text went to press before the end of rehearsals and so may
differ slightly from the play as performed.

Scene One

A large sunny room in MIKHAIL GORBACHEV's *Presidential dacha, a very substantial building overlooking the Black Sea. The room contains sofas, easy chairs, tables, etc. A little girl, Anastasia (called* NASTENKA), *is standing in front of a full-length mirror.* RAISA, *her grandmother, kneels beside her pinning up the hem of the peasant-style dress she is trying on.*

RAISA. There. Do you like that?

NASTENKA. Yes.

RAISA. Really, really?

NASTENKA. Yes.

RAISA. Good. Now turn round so I can do the back.

> NASTENKA *does so.*

NASTENKA. Can I wear it for my party?

> *She fidgets.*

RAISA. Only if you stand still. It won't be finished otherwise.

NASTENKA. Mummy said it's very old.

RAISA. These bits are. (*She points to various panels.*) The embroidery. An old lady gave them to me when I visited her village. She made them herself.

NASTENKA. Was she a witch?

RAISA. Of course not. But she was very old and she sewed all those stitches when she was just a little girl. And now she wants someone else to have it and to enjoy it, to keep the tradition going. So she gave it to me, for you.

NASTENKA. Did you say thank you?

RAISA. Yes I did. And so must you. We'll take a picture of you wearing the dress and you can write a letter to go with it and we'll send them to her. Will you do that for me, Nastenka, write a letter?

NASTENKA. Yes, Granny.

RAISA. Good girl. Now let's get this off. (*She starts to take the dress off.*) And you must go upstairs to your mummy and your sister because it's nearly time for your tea.

NASTENKA. Will you come swimming with us tomorrow – before we go home?

RAISA. I might, if there's time.

NASTENKA. Will you?

RAISA. If you want me to, yes. Come on now, off you run.

NASTENKA. Bye bye, Granny.

RAISA. Bye bye.

> NASTENKA *goes.* RAISA *moves the mirror back to its proper place then sits down to her sewing.* MIKHAIL *enters. He is eating chocolate drops.*

Hello.

> *She holds up the dress for inspection.*

What do you think?

MIKHAIL. Very good.

RAISA. Nastenka likes it. She just tried it on.

MIKHAIL. And I missed her.

RAISA. I thought you'd be too busy for children.

MIKHAIL. I'm never too busy for children. Anyway, I've finished.

RAISA. I don't believe you.

MIKHAIL. I have. Speech done. Every last dot and comma.

RAISA (*teasing*). And you won't change it? Not one tiny little tweak or fiddle? Not one adjective, not one little phrase?

MIKHAIL. No.

RAISA. Not a tiny half-sentence, a single little adverb?

MIKHAIL. Not a jot.

RAISA. Well, congratulations.

MIKHAIL. I hope. I hope. It'll be one of the hardest speeches of my life.

RAISA. Nonsense, it's all been agreed.

MIKHAIL. Only after hours of wrangling.

RAISA. You'll make a wonderful speech, then all those fat men in grey suits will unfurl their fountain pens and sign on the dotted line just like they said they would. It's a formality.

MIKHAIL (*unconvinced*). Yes.

RAISA. Yes.

MIKHAIL. 'What we will achieve today with the signing of this historic Union Treaty, is what our people have been waiting for . . . '

RAISA. Is this what you're going to say?

MIKHAIL. Yes. (*He orates*.) 'People in snowy Khabarovsk seven thousand miles away, people in mountainous Irkutsk scarcely less far, people in the Steppe-land city of Omsk, in windy Riga, in steamy Odessa . . . people all over our vast and beautiful land who have had to turn their faces to Moscow to await decisions on their lives, will breathe a sigh of relief – and draw in a new breath of freedom. Now, at last, power has come home, to them and to their republics – to elect their own leaders, to order their own region, and to do so still, as ever, as part of our United Soviet federation. Sharing in equality, in security and in hope.'

RAISA. And then there'll be a standing ovation – and you'll be a hero.

MIKHAIL. I don't need to be that, I just want it to happen.

RAISA. It will.

MIKHAIL. Then what? Enemies lining up on both sides.

RAISA. They'll cancel each other out, you said so.

MIKHAIL. I said I hoped they would.
    (*He looks at the dress again.*) That's from Georgia, isn't it?

RAISA. The embroidery is, yes. A village outside Batumi.
    Traditional work.

MIKHAIL. Will it be finished by Tuesday?

RAISA. Should be.

MIKHAIL. Then Nastenka must wear it for the day of the
    Treaty. And Izvestia can print a picture of her. 'President's
    granddaughter sports an example of the traditional crafts of
    the Republic of Georgia.' Every republic respected, every
    republic equal.

RAISA. Not turning into a politician are you?

MIKHAIL. It's fair enough – the hours you've spent tramping
    the villages.

RAISA. Tadzhomi, that's the name – the place the embroidery's
    from. I put it in my PhD. I used to show my students photo-
    graphs – it's still got all the old carved door-posts.

MIKHAIL. I love the way you love it.

RAISA. I do. It's the people's history.

    She points to a woven picture on the wall.

    Do you like my owl?

MIKHAIL. Where did that spring from?

RAISA. He's from Azerbaijan. I brought him down from
    Moscow so at least he'll feel nearer home. Anyway, he
    brightens up the room.

MIKHAIL. I'm sorry this house is so official.

RAISA. It's too big, that's all. Staff quarters, guards quarters
. . . it never feels like a place for a holiday.

MIKHAIL. Presidents aren't allowed holidays.

RAISA (*lightly*). Or don't choose to take them.
(*Indicating owl.*) Wisdom and tranquillity, that's what he
stands for.

MIKHAIL. I could do with some of that.
It's alright, isn't it, the speech?

RAISA. Yes. Would you like some tea?

MIKHAIL. Tea?

RAISA. Tea. You know, tea?

MIKHAIL. I'm sorry, I've just thought of something I need to
add. I'll be back in a minute.

He makes for the door. She raises her eyes to heaven – affectionate exasperation.

RAISA. I'll be on the veranda.

*She walks out, carrying her sewing, onto the adjoining
veranda which overlooks the sea. She sits on a summer chair
and admires the view in the warm late afternoon sunshine. She
puts her sewing to one side and picks up a book. She is quickly
immersed in it . . . turns a page . . . reads on . . . tranquillity.*
MIKHAIL *returns to join her. He is eating sweets again.*

MIKHAIL. Told you I'd only be a moment.

RAISA. Satisfied?

MIKHAIL. Yes. You look very happy.

RAISA. I am. I could stay out here for ever.

MIKHAIL. With your head in a book.

RAISA. As long as I have that, I don't miss a thing.

MIKHAIL (*teasing*). Not even the joys of the Kremlin?

RAISA. Specially not the Kremlin.

MIKHAIL. You can't change things standing on a beach, that's the trouble.

RAISA. Oh, I don't know.

MIKHAIL. The soul maybe. Not wheat quotas.

RAISA (*humour*). Ah, wheat! Never far from your thoughts.

MIKHAIL. We've got to stop importing the stuff.

RAISA. Tomorrow. Now it's our last day, so just look at the sea.

There is a pause as MIKHAIL *gazes out. It calms him.*

MIKHAIL. . . . When I first saw that, I cried. I did. It felt like home. Cloud shadows chasing over it . . . wind . . . just like the Steppe. They say that, don't they? A blue Steppe.

She smiles at him.

RAISA. 'Plough', ploughing the land, is from the Greek word for ship – because the plough moves through the soil like a ship through the sea. Nice, isn't it.

MIKHAIL. What a scholar! (*He takes her hand.*) Tonight, we'll watch the sunset. Hand in hand. Promise.

RAISA *looks up at him, full of love.*

Right down to the last peep, when his head goes under the sea, like you like.

He drops her hand.

But first I just have to –

RAISA. Again?

MIKHAIL. Final phone calls. Must make sure everything's set for the journey. Then I can relax. Read your book – I won't be long.

He goes. She resumes her reading again. Peace. Then suddenly MIKHAIL *is back. He stands in silence, looking grim, preparing to speak.*

RAISA. What is it?
   . . . ?
   What? What is it?

MIKHAIL. The phones have been cut off.

She stares at him in alarm.

They've cut off the phones.

RAISA. Who have?

He shakes his head – doesn't know.

Maybe they're just not working.

MIKHAIL. They've been severed. Everything has. Radio, television . . . nothing works. I've tried.

RAISA. It's a power cut.

MIKHAIL. And there are five men standing down in the hallway demanding to see me. Demanding.

RAISA. Who? Who are they?

MIKHAIL. I don't know. Our guards let them in because Plekhanov was with them, so they thought it was alright. They're from Moscow.
   This is it, Raisa. It's happening.

RAISA. Where's Irina?

MIKHAIL. I'll go up and get her. And Tolya. Then we must decide what to do.

Scene Two

Back in the big room about ten minutes later. RAISA *is pacing about.* ANATOLY, *their son-in-law, enters.*

ANATOLY. What's up? He looks grim.

RAISA. Wait. Just wait.

> *A moment or so later* MIKHAIL *enters. He is guiding* IRINA, *their daughter – his hand on her shoulder.*

MIKHAIL (*to* IRINA). It'll be alright, you're not to worry.

IRINA. I'm not. I just want to *know*.

MIKHAIL. I'll tell you everything in a minute. Go on, you sit there.

> *He indicates a sofa where she and* ANATOLY *are to seat themselves together.*

> RAISA *has come to him and is stroking him anxiously.*

And you, Raya, sit down. All of you.

> *They all sit.*

Now.
I'm sorry I've called you in here like this so suddenly. But I can't help it. Something has happened. (*A blank pause.*) And we have to decide what to do.
A delegation has arrived from Moscow. Five men. I've found out who they are now – four Central Committee, and some Army General. They want to see me, and I don't think they've come with a bunch of flowers.

IRINA. There was a soldier with a rifle in the hall. Not one of your guards.

MIKHAIL. Yes, I saw him.

IRINA. He looked very . . .

MIKHAIL. Yes, I'm sorry. We'll take care of all that. I promise.

ANATOLY. So why are they here?

MIKHAIL. I think they've been sent to make demands. And to stop me. . . . Stop the reforms.

ANATOLY. So it's the conservatives?

MIKHAIL. Yes.

ANATOLY. Well, they're too late, aren't they.

MIKHAIL. Rather depends what they have in mind. I expect they'll start by asking me to withdraw the Treaty, and when I won't, they'll 'ask' me to resign. And when I won't, they'll . . . try something else.

ANATOLY (*a sort of black joke*). Like shooting you?

IRINA. Don't.

MIKHAIL. Well yes, that's always a possibility. But I don't think so.
Yet.

ANATOLY. It'll be blackmail, won't it, first. Arm twisting.

MIKHAIL. Yes. And I will resist. I want you to know that. Whatever happens, I will resist.

Silence.

IRINA. You're very brave.

ANATOLY. You might be wrong. They might have just come to discuss things.

MIKHAIL. Then why not wait till tomorrow when I'm in Moscow?

RAISA. Why cut off the phones?

IRINA. The phones? So you can't ring Boris or –

MIKHAIL. No. No one.

ANATOLY. You're right. It's serious.

MIKHAIL. So we need to decide what to do. If things go badly, you may not be able to leave later. So if you want to move to safety now, I think you should.

IRINA. My children.

MIKHAIL. Yes, you must put them first. If you'd like to go, I'll call Plekhanov and arrange it. You'll have my blessing.

IRINA *doesn't answer.*

Well, Irina? I'm asking you first because you have the most at risk. I think perhaps you should go. It would make me feel easier.

IRINA (*with resolution*). No. I won't go.

MIKHAIL. Not for the children?

IRINA. No. We'll take care of them here and I'll stay. You're my father and you're the President. I won't desert you.

MIKHAIL. You're sure? Absolutely?

IRINA. Yes.

MIKHAIL. Well, thank you.

IRINA (*trying to lighten the strain*). Anyway, I'm a doctor. You must have a physician with you.

MIKHAIL (*trying to keep light*). Let's hope I won't need one, eh.
(*Turning to* ANATOLY.) Anatoly?

IRINA. None of us will desert you.

MIKHAIL. Anatoly?

ANATOLY. Of course I'll stay. I couldn't be less brave than my wife, now could I!

MIKHAIL. Raya?

RAISA. You don't have to ask. I'll stay. Always and for ever. I couldn't be less brave than my husband, now could I.

MIKHAIL. Thank you. Thank you all.

> RAISA *rises and embraces him. The others join. He puts his arms round them all and they stand in a joint embrace.*

My family. My loyal, beautiful family. I love you.

He breaks away.

Now. I better call the intruders to my office and we'll see what happens. I'll be back.

He goes.

ANATOLY. He hopes.

RAISA. Don't, Tolya! Just don't.

Echo One

Sound tape insert played through speakers:

Ghostly, barely distinguishable sounds of a family – that of CZAR NICHOLAS II *in 1917 – being ushered into an echoing room in a commandeered house in Yekaterinberg where they are to be held prisoner. Footsteps on wooden stairs, then feet on floorboards. The rustling of long dresses. Voices very muffled and unclear. It could be quite good that the audience don't really know what this is yet.*

GUARD. This is it.

OLGA. Oh, Papa!

NICHOLAS. Sshh!

GUARD. You will stay here, all of you. Alright.

Door shuts on them.

Scene Three

Later, the contemporary, Black Sea room. RAISA, IRINA *and* ANATOLY *are sitting. Waiting. They have been there some time.*

ANATOLY. How much longer?

    RAISA *silently shakes her head.*

    It's been nearly an hour.

RAISA. An hour to overthrow a president and destroy a life's work? It doesn't seem long to me.

ANATOLY. That won't happen.

RAISA. No. Why did I say it.

ANATOLY. He'd rather be shot.

RAISA. Thank you, Anatoly.

ANATOLY. Well, I mean . . .

RAISA. I know what you mean.

IRINA. My father is very strong. I believe in him.

ANATOLY. We all do.

RAISA. Then let's try to show it.

IRINA. We are. We're with him.

RAISA. They can't make him resign. Can they?

ANATOLY. 'The Politburo thinks . . . ', 'The Supreme Soviet has warned . . . ', 'Fall on your sword for the good of the Party . . . '

RAISA. Like under Stalin.

ANATOLY. They've got form alright.

RAISA. They're wrong. Wrong.

ANATOLY. He's playing a dangerous game.

RAISA. It's not a game, it's life and death to him.

ANATOLY. Raisa, I know. I know.

RAISA. Come on, we can't just sit here. We must be positive. *Do* something!

She gets up restlessly. Goes to the window.

Oh my God. Look!

ANATOLY. What?

He comes to the window.

RAISA. Dozens of soldiers. With machine guns.

ANATOLY. They're not Mikhail's guards?

IRINA *comes to the window.*

RAISA. No, new. They must have come with the delegation. They're like ants.

IRINA (*pointing*). That's the one I saw in the hall.

RAISA. We're prisoners.

IRINA. But they can't just . . . [imprison us.] He's the President.

ANATOLY. They can do what they want.

IRINA (*sudden panic*). I must find the girls.

Rushing toward the door.

I must find my children.

ANATOLY. Irina, be careful! There are –

He rushes after her.

RAISA is left alone. The evening light is dimming a little. She paces, desperately. She sits down, restless.

After a pause, the door opens. MIKHAIL *ushers in* PLEKHANOV.

MIKHAIL. You better come in.

RAISA (*moving toward* MIKHAIL). Mikhail!

MIKHAIL. It's alright, Raya. I'm alright.

He signals her to hold off then turns to PLEKHANOV.

(*Offering* PLEKHANOV *the benefit of the doubt about his actions*.) Now, Yuri, you better explain yourself.

PLEKHANOV. Explain.

MIKHAIL. Yes, I want an explanation – of how you came to let them in. (PLEKHANOV *looks blank*.) The 'delegation'.

No answer.

Well . . . ?
Well, was it some kind of mistake?

PLEKHANOV. No, it wasn't a mistake.

MIKHAIL. Not a mistake?

PLEKHANOV. No.

MIKHAIL *takes this in.*

MIKHAIL. So you intended this. You knew about it.

PLEKHANOV. Yes.

MIKHAIL. You, a senior officer of the KGB, you, head of my security, in charge of my personal safety, you led in a group of conspirators whom you knew were planning to oust the rightful President, oust *me*, from my seat.

PLEKHANOV. Mikhail, I –

MIKHAIL. Yes or no?

PLEKHANOV. Yes.
Mikhail, I believe –

MIKHAIL (*his restraint breaks, a sudden explosion*). I don't care what you believe! I don't care. Just get out of my sight. Out! You traitor. You bastard. You shit. Out! Out! Out!

PLEKHANOV (*protesting as he is bundled out of the door*).
Mikhail, I –

MIKHAIL. Fuck you!

MIKHAIL slams the door on him.

Then he puts his head in his hands.

Pause as he recovers himself.

I'm sorry.

RAISA. He deserved it. Every inch.

MIKHAIL. The head of my security opened the doors and led
in the conspirators who are trying to overthrow me. He
betrayed me.

RAISA. He'll burn in hell. I'll light the fire.

Pause.

Mikhail, what happened?
. . . Mikhail? What did they say?

MIKHAIL. A minute. Just give me a minute.

*Perhaps he crosses the room, or sits. She comes towards him
but he's still rebuilding. She understands – gives him a little
longer till he looks ready.*

RAISA. Do you want me to call Irina now and . . . ?

MIKHAIL. No . . . No.

RAISA. They went to find the children.

MIKHAIL. The children will be alright. At least for now.

RAISA. Tell me what happened.

MIKHAIL. Unspeakable. All of it.

Her look prompts him.

They've set up some committee.

RAISA. Who have?

MIKHAIL. Baklanov, Pavlov, the Vice President . . . It's not just the old guard but . . . half the people, half the people I appointed, half of them . . . they're betraying me too. They've set up a committee and they're going to declare a State of Emergency. It'll stop everything.

RAISA. They can't do that.

MIKHAIL. Well, they are. They're panicking. 'The economy's in chaos, and the Treaty will split the State apart' – that's what they say. Well, we've been through all this before – reforms take time. They just don't have the balls to keep at it.

RAISA. They're cowards and they're traitors, that's why! They don't know what's right for the country.

MIKHAIL. Then they told me if I wouldn't sign the Emergency – to make it all look legal – I had to resign.

RAISA *hisses angrily.*

When I refused, they started asking about my health. Very solicitous, they were – the workload, the strain . . . I thought it was a threat at first, but it was a bribe, a disgusting bribe – If I agreed that I was ill, my Deputy could sign the Decree and I could come back afterwards once the new policies were in place.

RAISA. The old ones, they mean.

MIKHAIL. Exactly. Everything shut down, reforms cancelled, back to Brezhnev, Stalin, even. Well, I promised our people something and I'll give it to them. I won't go back.

RAISA. I know that.

MIKHAIL. I won't.

Pause.

RAISA. So what happens now?

MIKHAIL. They return to Moscow – they've gone already, I saw the cars – they return to Moscow and . . . I suppose . . . they declare the Emergency anyway – without my signature. Oh, and they've arrested Yeltsin.

RAISA. No!

MIKHAIL. This morning. The President of the Soviet Union's greatest republic, the President of Russia no less, in custody.

Pause.

RAISA. So this really is a coup.

MIKHAIL. And we are prisoners. Yes. And they've left a lot of soldiers behind too.

RAISA. We saw them from the window.

MIKHAIL. With Plekhanov in charge. Just to keep an eye on us, of course. In case we try signalling from the rooftops. Fancy a bit of semaphore? I learned it as a boy in case of Germans. Or we could try smoke-signals – the Tartars were supposed to be good at that.

RAISA. At least we've got our guards.

MIKHAIL. Assuming they're still with us.

RAISA. They will be. Local boys. Loyal. That's what country life does for people. Your own little company of troops, and they love you. (*Reassuring.*) You know they do.

MIKHAIL. So I better find young Captain Klimov then, hadn't I?

RAISA. Our Oleg – someone to trust.

MIKHAIL. You should go and see Irina and Tolya and explain what's going on. There's no staff now, you know. I told them to go. Safer for them.

RAISA. That was kind.

MIKHAIL. Except the cook refused to leave. Won't desert us, she said.

RAISA. Kinder still. Brave old Galina.

MIKHAIL. And I'll try and get the guards to rig up some kind of radio aerial. That's the trouble – it's the aerials are gone, not the power. We must know what's happening in the outside world.

He starts to go.

RAISA. Oh Misha.

Echo Two

Ghostly echo of the Yekaterinberg room, as before. Voices perhaps a little clearer now.

ANASTASIA. Why have they painted over the windows?

OLGA. So we can't see out.

ALEXANDRA. We're prisoners, aren't we?

NICHOLAS. Yes. Yes, prisoners.

Scene Four

Late at night, same day, same room. ANATOLY is balancing precariously on a chair. He is attempting to hook a lot of makeshift bent wire – interlinked metal coat-hangers? – which trails back to a 'radiogram', onto a high light-fitting. His struggles are comic. RAISA stands by him, steadying his chair. MIKHAIL is seated, sorting through papers with fierce concentration and occasionally scribbling frantic notes.

RAISA (*to* ANATOLY). Do you really think this will work?

ANATOLY. Aerials are always metal, so . . .

RAISA (*as* ANATOLY *strains upward*). You're nearly there.

ANATOLY. If I can just . . . just . . .

He makes a final effort but misses the spot.

Fuck!

The whole lot clatters to the ground.

Fuck! Fuck! Fuck!

He climbs down from the chair and starts to gather up the debris.

RAISA. You tried.

ANATOLY. And failed. Again? (*i.e. Shall I try again?*)

MIKHAIL (*looks up from papers*). No, please.

ANATOLY. I know I'm disturbing you but –

MIKHAIL (*speaking over him*). It's alright, it's just –

ANATOLY. I know: hopeless.

RAISA. He didn't say that.

MIKHAIL. You're a surgeon, not an electrician. If Captain Oleg and his merry men can't do it, you can't.

RAISA. It was worth a try.

ANATOLY. It's alright, I'll go.

MIKHAIL. With Irina and the children – that's where you're needed most tonight.

ANATOLY. Yes, yes, you're right. She's doing well, you know. Very organised. Our floor upstairs will be kept as normal as possible, so the children feel safe. Proper bedtimes, proper mealtimes, and no running round the house and bumping into soldiers. Nothing unusual to frighten them. She's got it all worked out. You'd be proud of her.

RAISA. I am. And thank you, Tolya, for . . . (*She gestures toward aerial attempt.*)

ANATOLY. Oh . . . (*A shrug. Then a warm smile.*) Goodnight, Raya.
(*Nods goodnight to* MIKHAIL.) Mikhail.

MIKHAIL. Goodnight. And sleep well. If you can.

ANATOLY goes. MIKHAIL *resumes his scribbling.* RAISA *returns the chair to its proper place and then sits down.*

RAISA. You could be a bit more gracious. He was actually being positive for once.

MIKHAIL (*still scribbling*). Yes. Sorry.

RAISA *stares into space. She is trying to be calm but her fidgeting hands give her away.* MIKHAIL*'s frustration at what he is reading mounts.*

This is ludicrous! Look at this! A memo supporting my trade plan, signed by every one of those shits who are trying to overthrow me. Three weeks ago, that was. Three weeks! Look! (*He thrusts it at her.*)

RAISA. I know.

MIKHAIL. You can't trust anyone. I had a phone call from Yanayev this morning, *this morning*, saying he'd meet me at Moscow airport. He knew bloody well I'd be banged up here surrounded by machine guns – it was he who ordered it!

He stuffs a handful of his chocolate buttons into his mouth and chews frantically.

RAISA. Please calm down. You'll make yourself ill.

MIKHAIL. Someone else worried about my health now.

RAISA. I'm sorry. I'm sorry, but . . .

MIKHAIL (*sighs*). I know. So am I.

RAISA *watches him.*

RAISA. Please stop working. It's not doing you any good.

MIKHAIL. It's not about *me*.

RAISA. I know, I mean . . . Please, Misha.

MIKHAIL (*a pause*). Yes, yes, you're right.

RAISA. You're too tired.

There's a tramping of heavy boots.

What's that!?

MIKHAIL. Just more of Plekhanov's soldiers, I expect.
They've put him in charge of the Frontier Unit – that lot
out there. He's supposed to be KGB, not commanding a
bloody army.

RAISA. They'll be prosecuted when it's over.

MIKHAIL. If we ever get that far.

RAISA. We will. Because we are right.

MIKHAIL (*very sincerely*). You're still a believer, aren't you.
Thank God someone is.

RAISA. Come on, my darling, come and sit with me.

RAISA indicates the sofa. He sits. There's some calm.

MIKHAIL. We missed our sunset.

RAISA. There'll be others.
I bet your mother watched it. Out there in her little garden.
Shut the chickens up – even the white one she can never
catch . . . watered her roses . . . then she lent back against
that old birch tree and watched the sun go down. Just like
always. And now she's gone inside and had her supper and
she's thinking of bed. In the house your father built for her,
in the village you were born in, just like always. Door
locked, stove closed, light out. Peace.

MIKHAIL. Don't.

RAISA. Why? It's all still there. Life goes on as though nothing has happened.

MIKHAIL. It won't if we don't do something.

RAISA. In the morning, my darling. You need sleep. You used to sleep like a child.

MIKHAIL. Well, I'm grown up now.

RAISA. But your conscience is still clear.
Irina said the girls went down like lambs.

MIKHAIL. They don't understand what's happened, that's why.

RAISA. Nor do I. I can't quite believe it.

MIKHAIL. I can. Now. A lot's changed in the last few hours. Something's gone . . .

He doesn't go on.

RAISA. What?

MIKHAIL (*bleak*). Trust. I don't think I trust anyone any more.

RAISA. Don't say that.

MIKHAIL. I don't want to, but . . .

RAISA. Please. You're a good man, Misha. A good, good man. Open, generous . . . and trusting.

MIKHAIL. Am I?

RAISA. And you'll sleep, and you'll wake up and you'll face the world and carry on your work as you always did. I know you will.

Pause.

Shall I sing to you? Like the old days – when you came back tired from the fields . . . So tired you could hardly hold a cup . . .
(*About the song.*) The Ukrainian one about the girl at the spinning wheel.

She begins to sing a phrase or two of a folk song.

MIKHAIL. No. No. Stop.

RAISA. Why?

MIKHAIL. Because I can't bear it. I can't bear . . . the innocence of it.

Scene Five

Very early the next morning, Monday 19th August. Bright and sunny. MIKHAIL is gazing restlessly out of the window. RAISA rushes toward him brandishing a small transistor radio.

RAISA. Mikhail! Mikhail! Look what I've found! The Sony. It was under the bed.

MIKHAIL. I'd forgotten about it!

RAISA. So had I. I was looking for my shoe and –

MIKHAIL (*interrupting*). Does it work?

She turns it on. Static.

RAISA. Yes. Yes.

MIKHAIL. Can you find a station? Some news.

She scans the dial. Picks up a Russian station – music, Swan Lake, *loud and clear.*

That'll be us. The state solution when there's an emergency – play *Swan Lake*! What about the BBC, the World Service?

Suddenly there is a knock on the door.

Hide it. Quickly.

She hastily stuffs it under a cushion. More knocking.

ANATOLY (*outside the door*). It's me, Tolya. Can I come in?

MIKHAIL. Of course. Of course, come in.

ANATOLY (*entering*). Am I too early? You see –

MIKHAIL. It's alright, the holiday's over.

ANATOLY. You see, there are warships in the bay, I just saw them and I thought you should know, so I –

MIKHAIL. We do know. Raisa saw them. At about five.

ANATOLY (*slightly crestfallen but joking*). Failed again! Just when I thought I could be useful.

RAISA. I couldn't sleep, that's all.

ANATOLY. Irina said I should come down. She's very keen I should be at your service. So . . .

MIKHAIL. Thank you. And thank you for last night – the aerial.

ANATOLY. Hardly a success.
So what about the warships? What do they mean?

RAISA. Maybe we can find out. Look – (*Produces the Sony with a flourish.*) – We have news! Or might have.

RAISA *turns it on. It blares loud music.*

MIKHAIL. Turn it down! They'll hear us.

She does so. She continues to scan dial at a much lower level.

It means the place is blockaded, that's all. We're prisoners. Land and sea.

RAISA *finds the World Service.*

ANATOLY (*over first few words from radio*). That's the BBC. (*Looks at his watch.*) It should be time for the news.

As the sound fades up to full, it crosses from transistor to come from the stage speakers, like the 'Echo' sequences.

RADIO. . . . television and radio have broadcast a decree declaring a national State of Emergency –

MIKHAIL (*over the radio*). There, I told you.

RADIO. – The decree issued on behalf of the 'Soviet leader-ship', stated that 'for reasons of health' President Gorbachev is incapable of carrying out his duties and Vice President Yanayev will assume the functions of the President. An eight-man Emergency Committee has been formed to admin-ister the country for six months during 'this period of crisis'. The exact whereabouts of President Gorbachev are currently unclear. We will bring you more news on this as soon as we have it. This is BBC World Service News . . .

Fades out as RAISA *turns radio off.*

Long pause.

MIKHAIL. Well, they've done it. A State of Emergency.

ANATOLY. And Yanayev a pretend president.

RAISA (*fearing a threat*). For 'reasons of health', they said, Misha.

MIKHAIL (*suddenly*). This is intolerable,
(*To* ANATOLY.) Call Plekhanov. I have something to say to him. *I* do! On behalf of the people.

ANATOLY. You want him now?

MIKHAIL. Yes, now! At once! Here, take this. (*He grabs the radio from* RAISA *and thrusts it at* ANATOLY.)
Hide it. If Plekhanov's men find it we've lost our lifeline. And keep monitoring it.
Now get Plekhanov!

ANATOLY *goes out hastily.* RAISA *stares at* MIKHAIL *dumbly.*

I was rude to him. I'm sorry.

RAISA. It isn't that.

MIKHAIL. If I can't be respectful to those I love then what hope is there.

RAISA. Do you want me to be here when Plekhanov comes?

MIKHAIL. No. No.

RAISA. Probably just as well. I couldn't keep my temper.

MIKHAIL. I'm not sure I will.

RAISA. You're better at it than me. It's why you're the politician.

MIKHAIL. Why don't you go and see the children. Irina will appreciate it.

RAISA. She seems to be coping, doesn't she. But she won't find it easy.

MIKHAIL. None of us do.

   RAISA *kisses his cheek. He grips her hand in a squeeze of support. Just as she is about to go, there is a knock at the door. They exchange looks.*

   Come in.

   PLEKHANOV *enters. Rather ridiculously, he is holding a large cake on a plate. He hovers a little nervously.*

PLEKHANOV. Good morning, Mikhail. Raisa Maximovna. (*Inclines his head to her.*)

RAISA (*cold*). Good morning, Comrade Plekhanov.

PLEKHANOV. I trust you slept well.

RAISA (*she makes a dismissive sound*). I'm going to see my grandchildren.

PLEKHANOV. I want you to know they'll be quite safe. Please give them my best wishes. And tell little Nastenka and Kseniya that I've brought them –

RAISA (*interrupting, completely ignoring the cake*). I don't think I'll tell them anything, Comrade.
Now will you let me past.

   She goes.

   Pause.

PLEKHANOV *still hovers awkwardly.* MIKHAIL *stares blankly at the cake.*

MIKHAIL. What's that?

PLEKHANOV. It's a cake.

MIKHAIL. I can see that.

PLEKHANOV. It's for the children. A present. A treat. I thought they might like it, but . . . Well, I just wanted them to know that . . . (*He gives up.*)

MIKHAIL. Put it down.

PLEKHANOV *looks round helplessly.*

MIKHAIL *coldly declining to rescue him in any way.*

Put it down, Yuri. Over there. Just put it down.

PLEKHANOV *finds somewhere. He returns to* MIKHAIL.

(*Flatly.*) Thank you.

PLEKHANOV. So. You wanted me?

MIKHAIL. No, but you're all I've got. Sit down.

He does. MIKHAIL *surveys him for some moments, in silence.*

I take it I have still got you, up to a point. You are still responsible for my safety? – the President's safety? – and I am still the President?

PLEKHANOV. Yes.

MIKHAIL. So you admit that. Despite having joined my enemies –

PLEKHANOV. I –

MIKHAIL (*interrupting*). – The country's enemies.

PLEKHANOV. I am doing my duty.

MIKHAIL. You are not.

PLEKHANOV. It's judged that your policies endanger the people's safety and the state's, so I –

MIKHAIL. By whom is it judged?

PLEKHANOV. By the Emergency Committee.

MIKHAIL. Which is illegal.

PLEKHANOV. The safety of the state comes before the law.

MIKHAIL. The safety of the state is dependent on the law. Break that principle and you have arbitrary power – totalitarianism. That is precisely what I am trying to lead us away from. And the people support me.

PLEKHANOV. Not any more.

MIKHAIL. Because you are bringing tanks onto the streets?

PLEKHANOV. We won't do that.

MIKHAIL. Good.

PLEKHANOV. This isn't a military coup, Mikhail. It's all by the book. Our Emergency announcement stated that, in accordance with Article 1277 of the Constitution, we –

MIKHAIL (*interrupting*). It's in accordance with nothing and you know it. This is a coup.

PLEKHANOV. Have you been harmed?

MIKHAIL. Harmed!?

PLEKHANOV. Harmed. No. Your movement is restricted and so is your guards', that's all. We haven't shot anyone, your guards are still free to serve you. As long as they behave peaceably we will respect them. We haven't even disarmed them.

MIKHAIL. Hardly necessary – with thirty of them against three hundred of you.

PLEKHANOV. I'm sorry you see it like that.

MIKHAIL. It's the truth.

PLEKHANOV. The truth is that the country is out of control and they are looking to us to restore order.

MIKHAIL. And does that involve propagating lies?

PLEKHANOV. What?

MIKHAIL. Lies. I gather your 'Committee' has made a public broadcast stating that I am so ill I am incapable of carrying out my duties. That is a lie. It is, isn't it. Answer me. Is that a lie?

Pause.

PLEKHANOV. Yes, Mikhail, it is.

MIKHAIL. So, Yuri Sergeyevich, you 'restore order' by telling the people lies. You betray your office.

PLEKHANOV. There are times when lying is necessary.

MIKHAIL. Oh, just like breaking laws then – another aspect of your duty you can conveniently dispense with at will.

PLEKHANOV. It is not at will, it –

MIKHAIL. Don't interrupt me! You are an officer of the KGB. I respect the KGB. I have worked with them – not because I like men in black mackintoshes trailing innocent citizens, but because I hate corruption and I want to stamp it out. To make our country decent again –

PLEKHANOV. Do you think I don't?

MIKHAIL (*silencing him with a look*). I want a place where ordinary people work hard and can be open and honest and not one where it's easier to keep quiet and do nothing because every effort you make is thwarted by a bureaucracy worse than Byzantium. I want one where we work together, not one run by fat officials who watch you wade through the mud because the road money is in their own pocket. Like the housing money, and the tractor money, and the fuel money. I want to make things better for people. And I thought you did too. I thought we shared a vision.

PLEKHANOV. We did.

MIKHAIL. So what went wrong?

Pause. He looks at PLEKHANOV *for a long time.*

Yuri, we're the same age, we've had the same lives. We know what needs to be done. So let's do it.

PLEKHANOV. Mikhail, I . . . (*He falls silent.*)

MIKHAIL. Why have you deserted me? You're not just any KGB man, you're the one I look to for my safety. It's your men who ride beside me to the Kremlin, and stand around me in a crowd. You're my protectors, not my gaolers. My own guards – the ones down here – are still loyal to me, but you are not. And you're the special one – the one nearest me, whom I talked to at the airport on the way to Washington, the one I sat with late at night – remember? – waiting for news from Chernobyl. You. And we agreed that things had to change. So what's gone wrong?

PLEKHANOV. Your policies, Mikhail. They don't work.

MIKHAIL. Give them time and they will.

PLEKHANOV (*shakes his head*). No, Mikhail.

MIKHAIL. We had to break the cycle! You know we did! You just can't run everything from the top, the whole machine grinds to a halt. You know, I sat in a Politburo meeting one day and they were discussing regulations for ladies' underwear! Senior Comrades from the Supreme Soviet – what kind of knickers are suitable for women working in the steel plants. Can you believe it!

PLEKHANOV (*perhaps finds it funny in spite of himself*). I'm not saying there hasn't been foolishness.

MIKHAIL. Foolishness!

PLEKHANOV (*after a pause, mischievously po-faced*). What did they decide? About the knickers?

MIKHAIL (*ignoring this*). We've been micromanaging everything from coke-smelting to the price of cabbages and it
can't go on. The people need freedom to make some of their
own decisions, run their own affairs. The ones on the ground
are the ones who know, and they should have their chance.

PLEKHANOV. Well, the ones on the ground can't cope. It's
chaos. In my old village the collective farm has been split up
and half the men are out of work. You can't even buy eggs
except on the black market.

MIKHAIL. If we wait, it will settle.

PLEKHANOV. If we wait, we'll end up with capitalism . . .
Capitalism, that's where you're going.

MIKHAIL. Socialism. Lenin's kind. The state hand in hand
with the people.

Pause.

PLEKHANOV. Do you really believe that?

MIKHAIL. Yes! Because capitalism is about greed. That's what
it's built on. Our state's not like that and never will be. We
know we're not here just for ourselves, for egotism, for *me*.
We have a sense of something beyond us. That's socialism.
We serve. Until capitalism, everyone did that – once it was a
god, or the king or the czar – even the old feudal lords saw
something nobler than their own pockets, even the boyars for
God's sake, knew more than bankers! 'I will not serve!',
wasn't that what the devil said? Because we have no gods here
any more, some people think we're devils, but we're not – we
leave that to the West! Now, here, with us, we serve the
people, the common good, each other. That's what I believe in,
it's what I'm trying to do. It means more to me than anything
and it comes from the soul. I've seen more joy in the faces of
people that serve and give and share than I've ever seen on the
face of some rich American in the West with a big car.

PLEKHANOV (*interrupting*). Mikhail, we know all this.

MIKHAIL. You don't, because you're trying to bring back
    tyranny! Giving only works if there's some freedom to it.
    People have to believe they're doing it freely. The self-respect
    of volition. We need a system and structure, yes, but control-
    ling people and cramping them and forcing them and watching
    them, only makes them mean. They lie and hide things and do
    the least. It's inefficient as well as wrong. And we've been
    there before.
    What I want is not capitalism, or selfishness, or self – it's gen-
    erous and good and it will make the people and the country
    strong. It's socialism, and we can build it and still be free.

Pause. PLEKHANOV *looks at him coolly.*

PLEKHANOV. Do you really never doubt yourself?

No answer.

Not at all, Mikhail?

No answer.

Because that's all just ideas.

MIKHAIL *turns his head in disgust.*

They sound nice, but it's not working.
Your freedom's creating chaos and we've stepped in to
correct it. This has been carefully planned.

MIKHAIL. Has it now. Well, I'd like to know a bit more about
    these plans. Maybe you could fill me in.

PLEKHANOV. I can't.

MIKHAIL. Because you don't know or because you don't care
    to tell me?

Silence.

Which? Because as the President, I'm quite keen to hear
what is happening to our country.

Pause.

No? Not so talkative now? Nothing to say?

PLEKHANOV. Discussing these things isn't my job.

MIKHAIL. Come, come, why so reticent all of a sudden?

PLEKHANOV. Times have changed.

MIKHAIL. They have indeed.

PLEKHANOV. Mikhail, why did you summon me here?

MIKHAIL. To make some demands, Yuri Sergeyevich. On behalf of the people.

PLEKHANOV. You better make them then.

MIKHAIL. As the duly elected President of the Union of Soviet Socialist Republics, sworn to protect and advance the peoples' welfare, I demand:
One, full restoration of all communications – that means telephones, radio, television, mail, newspapers, everything. And two, a plane back to Moscow. There is work to be done. I cannot leave the capital in the hands of criminals. You will transmit these demands. Will you? I order you to.

PLEKHANOV. Yes, Mikhail, I will. It is still my duty.

MIKHAIL. At least you've remembered some of it. Pity about the rest. Go.

PLEKHANOV. Mikhail –

MIKHAIL. I don't want to talk to you any more. Go.

To himself, as PLEKHANOV *shuts the door behind him.*

Get out of my sight.

Scene Six

Almost continuous from previous scene: the big room, as before.
MIKHAIL picks up the telephone. It's still dead. He replaces it.
He turns to his papers and sits down and starts writing. After a
while we hear the sound of children's voices and footsteps
approaching, then gentle taps on the door.

RAISA (*softly, outside the door*). Mikhail? Mikhail?

MIKHAIL. Yes, come in.

> RAISA *and* IRINA *with her two children,* KSENIYA *and*
> NASTENKA, *enter.*

RAISA. I wasn't sure he'd gone.

MIKHAIL. Yes, yes, he's gone.

RAISA. How did . . . ?

MIKHAIL. Later, later.

IRINA. I'm sorry, we shouldn't have come.

MIKHAIL. It's alright.

IRINA. It isn't really, but you see, the girls . . .

MIKHAIL. I said it's alright.

RAISA. Actually, I think we should go back upstairs. It was a
silly idea.

MIKHAIL. No, stay, please do. It'll take my mind off things.

RAISA. Are you sure?

MIKHAIL. A few minutes normality is no harm. Anyway, it's not
as though I've got much else to do. Under the circumstances.

IRINA. If you're sure. You see, the girls were so keen to see you.

MIKHAIL. And me to see them. Good morning, Kseniya.

KSENIYA. Good morning, Grandpa.

MIKHAIL. Good morning, Anastasia.

NASTENKA. Good morning, Grandpa.

MIKHAIL. Couldn't miss our little ritual, now could we. And how are you both? Did you sleep?

KSENIYA (*simultaneously*). No.

NASTENKA (*simultaneously*). Yes.

MIKHAIL. You never agree about anything, you two. I make it my life's work to bring harmony to the world and I can't even achieve it in my own family.
And you, Irina? You look tired.

IRINA. I'm fine.

He looks at her carefully, unconvinced.

Really I am.

MIKHAIL. Well, Kseniya, what are you planning for today?

KSENIYA. I don't like all these soldiers.

MIKHAIL. Nor do I, but we'll just have to put up with them for now.

KSENIYA. Why should we?

NASTENKA (*before* MIKHAIL *can answer*). I want to go swimming.

MIKHAIL. Do you now. We'll see.
(*To* IRINA.) Can she go? If we can still get onto our beach.

IRINA *hesitates*.

RAISA. I don't see why not. If our guards come with us.

IRINA. My children can't go swimming under armed guard.
(*She appeals to* MIKHAIL.) Please, Daddy, don't ask me.

MIKHAIL (*to* NASTENKA). Your mother thinks not.

NASTENKA. But I want to. I want to! It's still our holiday so you've *got* to let me go.

MIKHAIL. Normality, you see. Restored at once. And it takes you to do it, eh, my little Nastenka. So what shall we do instead?

NASTENKA. Swimming.

RAISA. Actually I think it might be a good idea to go outside. Then people round the headland will see us and know we're still alive.

IRINA. Alive!

RAISA. Yes, we don't want them to think – [we're dead.]

MIKHAIL (*signals her not to pursue this*). Please.

RAISA. Well, if we just disappear, people might believe –

MIKHAIL. Let's not discuss this now.

KSENIYA. I think we should discuss it. I want to know what's going on.

MIKHAIL. We're not entirely sure, Kseniya. But it won't be like this for long.

IRINA (*to* KSENIYA). See, I told you. Your grandfather's got everything in hand.

KSENIYA (*to* MIKHAIL). How do you know it won't be long?

MIKHAIL. Because I'm making plans. In the meantime, we better entertain ourselves. Come on.

KSENIYA. I'm not a child.

MIKHAIL (*an idea that might appeal*). How about a piece of cake? You'd like that, wouldn't you, Nastenka.

He brings over PLEKHANOV*'s cake.*

NASTENKA. Yes ple-ease.

KSENIYA. Where did you get it?

MIKHAIL. Comrade Plekhanov. A present.

RAISA. You accepted it?!

MIKHAIL. Yes. I . . .

RAISA. You shouldn't have.

MIKHAIL. For the children.

RAISA. Well, they can't have it.

NASTENKA. Oh please!

RAISA. No.

IRINA. No. If it's from Yuri Plekhanov, no.

RAISA (*to* MIKHAIL). You carry forgiveness too far.

MIKHAIL. I don't forgive him. He put it down, that's all, so I thought they might as well eat it.

RAISA. Well, they can't.

MIKHAIL. Alright. So . . . (*He casts about for something to do.*)
(*Inspiration: he turns to* NASTENKA.) Goodness, Nastenka, what's that you've got? Come here.

She does so.

Just look at you!

NASTENKA. What?

MIKHAIL. What's that? (*Pointing.*)

NASTENKA. Where?

MIKHAIL. There.

NASTENKA. Where?

MIKHAIL. Behind your ear.

NASTENKA (*feels*). There's nothing.

MIKHAIL. Yes there is. Look, a chocolate drop. (*Produces it.*)
Goodness, Nastenka, another one. And another one.

He produces sweeties from all over her. She starts giggling. More sweets, more laughter.

The girl's made of chocolate! Didn't you know? You bear it like a tree. Look at this. And this. They're everywhere. What a lot we've got.

He appears to have found a whole packet full in her pocket – planted by him – and is tossing them all around.

Enough for everyone. Can I have one? Can your sister have one? And your mummy and your granny? Yes? Come on, say yes.

NASTENKA. Yes.

MIKHAIL. Good girl. Always a sharer. Now one for you, eh. Open your mouth. (*She does and he gives her a sweet.*) And one for me.

He has one himself. RAISA *comes and puts her hands affectionately on his shoulders.*

See, it's not so bad here, is it.

NASTENKA. It's nice.

MIKHAIL. I told you.

He looks around, exhausted but at least pleased he's achieved something. They eat their sweets for a moment in silence, the children apparently content, though RAISA *and* IRINA *haven't lost their unease.*

Echo Three

Ghostly echoes from Yekaterinberg room as before. A child,
ALEXIS, *is giggling wildly, so is a girl,* ANASTASIA.

ALEXANDRA. That's enough now. Be careful with him. Sssh.
Remember that's the future Czar of Russia.

NICHOLAS. If we live that long.

The giggles subside.

The echo fades eerily to silence.

Scene Six (continued)

IRINA. I think we should go now. It's time to leave your
grandpa in peace.

NASTENKA. Now can I go swimming?

MIKHAIL. The girl's incorrigible.

A knock on the door interrupts them.

ANATOLY (*outside the door*). It's me, Tolya.

MIKHAIL. Come in.

ANATOLY does so. He scans the room.

ANATOLY. There's news – from the radio.

The others stare at him expectantly.

RAISA. What?

He pauses.

MIKHAIL. Perhaps you two girls really should be off. I'm
afraid we have a lot to do here. Do you mind, Kseniya? You
can look after Nastenka, can't you?

KSENIYA. I always get sent away when something interesting happens.

IRINA. I can't let them go by themselves.

MIKHAIL. Kseniya's a responsible girl. (*To* KSENIYA.) Aren't you?

KSENIYA. Yes.

RAISA. Yes. So – (*To* KSENIYA *and* NASTENKA.) Make sure you go straight up the stairs and straight to your room. Will you do that?

The girls nod.

Off you go.

IRINA. Alright.

She shepherds them to the door.

I'll be up as soon as I can.

They go. IRINA *returns reluctantly to the group.*

RAISA. They'll be fine.

MIKHAIL (*to* ANATOLY.) So, what's happened?

ANATOLY. Quite important, I think.

RAISA *stays very close to* MIKHAIL. *They are braced.*

According to the BBC – (*Wait for it.*) Yeltsin's still free. He was never arrested.

MIKHAIL. Are they sure?

ANATOLY. They seem to be.

MIKHAIL. So Baklanov was lying.

ANATOLY. And he has condemned the coup.

MIKHAIL. Yeltsin has?

ANATOLY. Yes. It said there were small demonstrations in Moscow and –

MIKHAIL (*interrupting*). Small?

ANATOLY. Small. And military vehicles outside buildings. Yeltsin jumped up on one and denounced the coup. What a showman, eh?

MIKHAIL. And they let him do it?

ANATOLY. Can't stop him really, can they. Get him shouting and it would take a cannon ball to shut him up.

IRINA. He's a brave man. I knew he was. (*To* MIKHAIL.) He'll fight for you, won't he?

MIKHAIL. I think so.

IRINA. He won't let you down. So he's our hope now, isn't he. Outside.

ANATOLY. As long as dear Boris remembers which side he's on.

RAISA. He's hardly with the plotters.

ANATOLY. You never know with him.

RAISA. Of course we know.

MIKHAIL. What kind of military vehicles?

ANATOLY. 'Including tanks', it said.

MIKHAIL. Dear God.

ANATOLY. But no trouble. No trouble . . . yet.

MIKHAIL. They've left Yeltsin alone because even they see that arresting him in his own city is too provocative. It's a good sign, they're being careful. With a following like his, they won't risk touching him. They don't want to be shooting into crowds if they can help it, not when they're posing as saviours, rather than murderers.

ANATOLY. They'll be murderers if they have to.

RAISA. Don't.

ANATOLY. Well, it's true.

RAISA. You don't have to say it.

ANATOLY. You do. *I* do. Then I'm prepared.

MIKHAIL. Anything else?

ANATOLY. That's all, I'm afraid.

MIKHAIL. It's enough to be going on with.

ANATOLY (*to* IRINA). Come on, we better go up to the children.

IRINA (*approaching* MIKHAIL). You mustn't worry about us – me and the children. I've got everything organised up there and I'll make sure they don't come down and interrupt you.

MIKHAIL. I like being interrupted.

IRINA. You're busy – and in danger. It's the whole world you're dealing with. You must conserve your strength, your health. I watch you and I know. You mustn't . . . you mustn't . . . (*She starts to break down a little.*) You can't be bothering about . . . [us.]

MIKHAIL (*puts his arm round her*). I can – bother about you. – I do. Oh my daughter, I do. I do. But it's all one, everything that happens outside and in, I don't divide it up. We're all in the same world.

IRINA (*recovering*). You are the President, a great man, and you mustn't be interrupted. I know that and I won't let it happen again.

IRINA *is together now.*

MIKHAIL. Go on, little one. Enough of this. Go up and find the children.
And I'll be fine. Order of the Red Banner of Labour, remember? I can do anything, three things at once! Promise. Alright?

IRINA. Yes. I'm sorry.

ANATOLY (*gently trying to guide her*). Come on, darling.

IRINA. Yes. Yes.

She looks back apprehensively as ANATOLY *leads her out.*

ANATOLY. Noah's coping fine.
(*Over his shoulder to* MIKHAIL *as he goes*.) As long as the
ark stays afloat.

The door closes.

RAISA (*after* ANATOLY *but not to him*). A pity we've got
Jonah on board then, isn't it. It's as though he enjoys being
a cynic.

MIKHAIL. He's not. Not really.

RAISA. You mean negativity helps? He's hardly a comfort.

MIKHAIL. I find him quite cheering actually.

RAISA *raises her eyes to heaven and gestures sarcastic
disbelief.*

Endearing, then. Because I know he doesn't mean a half of
it. It's his safety net.

RAISA. You see good in everybody.

MIKHAIL. Of course. So do you.

RAISA. He's alright, I know that. Of course he's alright.

MIKHAIL. And he loves our daughter from the bottom of
his heart.
Anyway, sometimes he might be right.

Pause.

RAISA. I didn't ask you how you got on with . . . That man.

MIKHAIL (*mock brightly*). The Traitor?

RAISA. 'Comrade' Plekhanov.

MIKHAIL (*reluctant, after a pause*). He . . .

RAISA. What? Tell me.

MIKHAIL. Yes. He . . .

RAISA. We face it together, Mikhail, always. United front.

Echo Four

Ghostly echo of Yekaterinberg, as before.

ALEXANDRA. At least the family is together.

NICHOLAS. But in what a place. (*He struggles in vain to force open a sealed-up window.*) Got to open this window . . . We've got to get some air!

ALEXANDRA. Just leave it. It's locked.
I told the girls to hide their medicines –

NICHOLAS (*still struggling*). It's like being criminals.

ALEXANDRA. – and to sew their jewels into their frocks.

NICHOLAS (*giving up*). No, no. I can't do it.

Echo fades.

Scene Seven

Afternoon of the same day. RAISA *is on the veranda. She looks out then turns and goes in.* MIKHAIL *is pacing about. Restlessly, he picks up the phone to check if there's a connection. There isn't.* RAISA *watches him.*

RAISA. It's not getting better, is it. I went out for a breath of freedom but it didn't feel like it. It's weirdly quiet, everyone's vanished. Except for the men with guns.

MIKHAIL. They've blocked off the road, that's why. Not just the lorry on the gates now, they've put checkpoints all the way along. According to the guards, the entire headland's sealed off.

RAISA. Wonderful!

And here we are trying to preserve normality. Did you hear Irina telling Nastenka to sit up straight at lunch? And she told me off because I was five minutes late.

MIKHAIL. She's trying to keep up standards.

RAISA. Oh, I'm all for it. It's just . . . well, they seem to be slipping a bit in the outside world, don't they.

MIKHAIL, *still restless, approaches the cake which is left on a side table. He starts to pick a bit off.*

No!

MIKHAIL (*annoyed*). Oh really!

RAISA. Eat chocolate drops if you must. Not that.

MIKHAIL. It's just a bloody cake.

He stuffs a handful of chocolate buttons in his mouth instead.

RAISA. Anyway, Irina says you eat too many sweet things. It's bad for you.

MIKHAIL (*raising his eyes to heaven*). Doctors!

Pause.

RAISA. So did you go back to him again? The cakeman?

MIKHAIL. Yes. Before lunch.

RAISA. And?

MIKHAIL. And what.

RAISA. Any response to this morning's demands?

MIKHAIL. They don't deign to reply.

RAISA. Damn them. Damn every one of them. And that man shares a name –

MIKHAIL (*interrupting*). Yes, ironic, isn't it. Shares a name with Georgi Plekhanov, the subtlest of Marxists, the gentle revolutionary. No relation, clearly.

RAISA. What you told me he said . . . His cynicism. I can't bear it.

MIKHAIL. No.

RAISA. You mustn't think about it. Disgraceful.

Pause.

MIKHAIL. I told him to send the demands again. And to remind them just how dangerous all this is. Protesters and tanks are a lethal combination.

RAISA. The people are our best hope. But . . .

MIKHAIL. Yeltsin could give them a real fright. My guess is they're running scared. They may want to be like Stalin but they haven't got –

RAISA. – the balls.

MIKHAIL. Exactly.

RAISA. Sitting in their polished offices clutching their bottles of vodka and –

MIKHAIL. – scared of what will happen next. Wondering if they'll have the courage to . . . to take the final step.

RAISA. You can't say it. Nor can I.

MIKHAIL. They're wondering if they'll have the courage to kill me. (*Sudden bark of a laugh.*) And they claim it's me who's ill! Yanayev's hand shakes so much in the morning he can't hold his first glass of vodka.

There's a knock on the door.

RAISA. That'll be Irina.

MIKHAIL. You were expecting her?

RAISA. Yes, well, you see . . .

She opens the door. IRINA *is standing there with a large holdall.* RAISA *helps her in with it. It is heavy.*

That's more than I thought.

IRINA. You don't know how long they might have to . . . to last out.

MIKHAIL. What's all this?

IRINA (*to* RAISA). Haven't you told him?

RAISA. No, not yet.

MIKHAIL. Told me what?

IRINA *sees the cake. She points at it in horror.*

IRINA. What's that doing there?! Why's that still there?!

MIKHAIL. What are you talking about?

IRINA. That's it! That's the point!

MIKHAIL. It's just a cake, Irina. The cake Yuri brought for the children. We'll get rid of it if you're so insistent. Though I must say I'm still tempted to have a bit.

He starts to pick at it.

IRINA *screams.*

IRINA. No!

MIKHAIL. What?

IRINA. It's poisoned! It's poisoned! You mustn't touch it.

MIKHAIL *looks bewildered – has she gone mad?*

Pause.

RAISA (*to* IRINA, *calm, quietly firm*). No really. I don't think so. Even *he* wouldn't do that.

IRINA. Yes. Kill my children. Didn't you listen to me? I was right, you know I was right. Everyone agreed – Oleg, the cook, everyone.

MIKHAIL. What is all this?

RAISA (*puts her arm round* IRINA, *calming her down*). Please, Irina.

IRINA *starts to breathe more easily.*

There. There.
I'll explain. It was Irina's idea and we all agree that she's
right. It's been decided that we shouldn't eat anything
brought into the house since the plotters came. Nothing that
wasn't here before they arrived. The guards have even
offered us their own supplies and the cook, our Galina, is
going to mark the safe stuff and keep it separate. We'll only
eat that. It's all arranged.

MIKHAIL. So you think they're going to poison me.

IRINA *nods grimly. She's calm again now.*

RAISA. Maybe.

MIKHAIL. It's possible. Neat and invisible. 'Natural causes.' A
Soviet speciality.

IRINA. I'm a doctor, I've seen what can happen. So you
mustn't eat the cake.

MIKHAIL. No. We'll throw it away.

He empties it decisively into the waste-paper basket.

There, see.

He looks at the holdall.

So what's all this?

IRINA. It's . . .

RAISA (*stepping in*). It's for the children. Dried fruit, nuts,
nourishing things. In case they have to . . . in case anything
happens to us and they have to fend for themselves. We're
going to hide it – we've worked it all out, Irina and I. It's
going to go in that cupboard and then we'll pull the screen
across and no one will even remember it's there.

MIKHAIL. You're quite something, you two, aren't you.

IRINA *carries the holdall across and opens the cupboard.*

RAISA. And we'll hide our medicines in there too. Anything we might need in case . . . of emergencies. It's all planned.

MIKHAIL. I sit here shuffling papers while you two women . . . What can I say? A pair of Zoyas, aren't you – the girl who saved her village from the Germans. (*There's humour here*.) 'Paragons of Soviet Womanhood!'

RAISA. We're trying, Misha.

MIKHAIL *moves affectionately towards* IRINA, *who is now standing on a chair and unloading her stores*.

MIKHAIL. Are you sure you're alright now?

IRINA *nods*.

Well done, my daughter.

IRINA*'s knees buckle. She faints and falls*.

Interval.

Scene Eight

The big room. 2 am – night of the same day. ANATOLY *and* RAISA *are busy setting things up to make a secret video of a speech by* MIKHAIL. *They draw the blinds and curtains to make a blackout, drag a chair and lamps to the centre, etc. Meanwhile,* MIKHAIL *is consulting his notes.* IRINA, *a bit tired and frail, is seated on a sofa swathed in a rug*.

IRINA (*as they're all busying themselves*). Why can't I help?

RAISA. Because you need to rest.

IRINA. I don't really.

ANATOLY. You do, my darling.

IRINA *sighs*.

RAISA (*at window*). Are you sure this blackout is alright?

ANATOLY. Yes.

RAISA. Sure, sure?

ANATOLY. Yes, not a chink of light. I checked it.

> RAISA *looks across at* MIKHAIL, *who is still correcting his notes.*

RAISA. He's rewritten that speech ten times, he'll be exhausted before he starts. What time is it?

ANATOLY. Ten past two.

RAISA. God, I was fed up with waiting!

ANATOLY. We had to be sure the house was quiet.

IRINA. There'll still be a night patrol.

RAISA. What about light under the door? I'll put something across it.

> *She hastens across the room, collects something serviceable – cushions? – then bustles back to fix the door, her burden only narrowly missing* MIKHAIL's *head as she passes. He ducks, irritated. Then she goes off to the bedroom.* ANATOLY *is dealing with the camera – his domestic camcorder.*

ANATOLY (*to* MIKHAIL). Nearly ready to go.

MIKHAIL (*preoccupied*). Mmm.

ANATOLY. Lucky there's enough tape. I was saving it to take Nastenka on the beach.

> RAISA *bustles back, carrying a shirt.*

RAISA (*to* MIKHAIL). I think you should wear this shirt.

MIKHAIL (*without looking up*). Mmm.

RAISA. Misha!

MIKHAIL. What?

RAISA. I think you should wear this.

He stares blankly.

It's a good positive colour. I washed it out specially.

MIKHAIL. What did you do that for?

RAISA. I have to do something, don't I. Anyway, that one (*re. the one he's wearing*) has got a spot. Look – there. Come on, I want you to change your shirt.

He makes no move.

Alright, I'll do it. (*She starts to unbutton his shirt.*)

MIKHAIL (*sudden rage*). Get off woman! For fuck's sake, just leave me alone!

RAISA (*backing off*). I'm sorry. I'm sorry.
I was only trying to help.

She exchanges glances with ANATOLY.

MIKHAIL (*sighing*). I'm sorry, I'm too tense to be civil.

They clasp hands for a second – reconciliation.

RAISA. It's the waiting. It's exhausted all of us.

MIKHAIL (*to* ANATOLY). Alright, I'm ready now.

He moves to the central chair and settles himself. RAISA *holds up a table lamp to give extra light for the camera.*

ANATOLY. Comfortable?

MIKHAIL. Yes.

ANATOLY (*lining up the shot*). OK. Go.

MIKHAIL. This is President Mikhail Sergeyevich Gorbachev speaking at two fifteen am on Tuesday the twentieth of August 1991.

I want everything I am about to say to be made known to the Peoples' Deputies of the USSR, to the Supreme Soviet of the USSR and to the Soviet public and the world.

You have been misled. You have been told that I, the President, am in bad health and unable to carry out my duties. As a result, the Vice President has taken over and a Committee of Emergency has been formed. I declare that everything said concerning my health is false. On the basis of a lie an anti-constitutional coup d'etat has been carried out. This house in the Crimea where I have been on holiday and from which I was due to fly today for the signature of the Treaty tomorrow, is surrounded by troops and I am under arrest. I am deprived of all government communications, all my telephones have been cut off and I have no contact with the world outside. Nobody is allowed to leave the territory of the dacha, I am surrounded by troops both on sea and land and I don't know if I shall succeed in getting this message out.

A crude deception is being carried out before your eyes. Most dangerous of all is that what the Committee of Emergency is doing may lead to an escalation of civil conflict and perhaps even to civil war.

People must act to solve problems, but we must follow the path of agreement not the path of conflict. Such conflict may have serious consequences not just for our own nation and people, but for the whole world.

That is what I wanted to say. I only ask you to evaluate it properly.

(*To* ANATOLY.) Alright?

ANATOLY. Yes. Got it.

RAISA. It was brilliant, Misha. You're brilliant.

MIKHAIL (*to* ANATOLY). Again?

ANATOLY. I'm afraid so. We agreed we've got to have four takes.

MIKHAIL *starts again. Perhaps a screen above the action shows a series of speeded up re-runs of the film. At the end, the focus switches back to* MIKHAIL *himself on stage.* ANATOLY *stops filming.* MIKHAIL *looks exhausted.*

You can relax now. Done.

RAISA. He's half dead with the strain, he must rest.

IRINA. Daddy, are you alright?

MIKHAIL. Yes, yes.

IRINA. Why did he have to do four? It's too much.

ANATOLY. We agreed – the more takes there are, the more chance one of them will survive –

MIKHAIL. Even if I don't!
I thought the speech about the Treaty would be the biggest of my life. Now I think this one might be.

ANATOLY. We've recorded the truth and we might even manage to smuggle it out. Then everyone will know and everything might change. If not, well . . . whatever happens, it will be here, for the future, waiting to be found.

MIKHAIL. It may be my epitaph.

RAISA. No. Not.

MIKHAIL (*humour*). 'The Death of a President.' Isn't there some film called that? We're getting as bad as America. How many have they shot?

ANATOLY. Oh, about half a dozen.

MIKHAIL. They're still ahead of us then. Even on that. I'll be our first.

RAISA *looks unimpressed*.

Sorry, that was my attempt at humour.

The sudden slam of a door, off.

RAISA. What's that?!

They listen in tense silent. Another slam.

I thought we'd checked the doors.

MIKHAIL. I better go and see.

RAISA. No, I'll go.

MIKHAIL. It's best if it's me.

RAISA. Then I'll come with you. I must come.

MIKHAIL. Alright. (*To* ANATOLY.) You stay and sort out the film.

> MIKHAIL *and* RAISA *go out.* ANATOLY *starts sorting his equipment. He's being quick about it in case anyone comes.*

IRINA. Do you think we've been discovered?

ANATOLY. No.
You should have stayed in bed. This is too much for you.

IRINA. I couldn't miss my father's speech. I couldn't. I couldn't.
What he says is right, I know it is. There could be a civil war.

ANATOLY. Yes.

IRINA. And I know he's the only one can stop it.

> ANATOLY *doesn't answer – he's concentrating on his camera equipment.*

Only him.

ANATOLY. Well . . .

IRINA. You don't believe it.

ANATOLY. He's not a god, Irina. He wouldn't be here if he were.

IRINA. He wouldn't be here if it weren't for cowards and plotters and traitors who aren't worthy to lick his boots. He's a great man.

ANATOLY. I know.

IRINA. Say it like you mean it!

ANATOLY. I do mean it, but I'm a realist. And I have to get on with this.

The camera is put away now and everything stowed. He begins to move the furniture back to its proper place. IRINA *rises to help.*

IRINA. I'll help.

ANATOLY. No, stay where you are. Please.

IRINA. I'm alright. I want to help.

She is up now. In haste, he pushes her back.

Ow!

ANATOLY. I'm sorry. I didn't mean to . . . [hurt you.]

He is torn between comforting her and moving the furniture.

IRINA. You don't think I'm strong enough.

ANATOLY. I do, but –

IRINA. But you have to get on with things. So do I.

She rises again and tries to help by lifting some item. She struggles with it and he hastens to rescue her.

ANATOLY. Sit down. Please sit down.

IRINA. No.

IRINA *battles on, determined to do it.*

ANATOLY (*he backs off*). Alright, alright. If you're sure.

IRINA. I am. – See.

IRINA *has the object in her grip now – and copes.*

They each continue to move stuff until the room is back to normal.

I can, see. I can. Believe me?

ANATOLY. I do love you, Irina. You don't have to . . . to be anything but yourself.

IRINA. I have to pull my weight. I don't want to be the little girl who gets put to bed because she can't cope.

ANATOLY. You'll never be that. But you're not well.

IRINA. I'm fine.

ANATOLY (*he touches her*). You are, you're shaking.

IRINA (*she touches him*). So are you.

ANATOLY (*he smiles*). I know. These terrible times.

She kisses him.

IRINA. I hope they come back soon. I'm going to help you cut up the tapes. Nimble little fingers, see. (*She waggles them.*) Perfect for the job.

ANATOLY. Alright. But first I have to check it's all there. Then I'll take the cassette apart and you can slice up the tape – four takes separate.

IRINA. And I'll put the cassette back together and no one will know it's been touched. My father's daughter, see – clever.

ANATOLY. Then we'll hide the bits – separately, safely.

IRINA. I've been thinking about that. There's a loose floorboard under our bed.

ANATOLY. Good. Yes.

IRINA. And we could unscrew the panel across the front of the bath and put one behind there.

ANATOLY. You have been thinking, haven't you.

IRINA. And Oleg said there's a place in the Guard Room. I don't know about the last one but I'll find somewhere. Anyway, it can be the one we smuggle out, can't it.

ANATOLY. If, if.

IRINA. Don't you think it's possible?

ANATOLY. Well, who? No one can leave.

IRINA. I thought maybe –

She's interrupted by a slight sound at the door. They look. It is opened very stealthily as MIKHAIL *and* RAISA *enter.*

ANATOLY. They're back.
(*To* MIKHAIL.) Alright?

MIKHAIL. Don't know what it was.

RAISA. No one in any of the corridors – we went right across
to the kitchens.

ANATOLY. We better be going now. We've work to do.

RAISA (*to* IRINA). Are you alright, little one?

IRINA. I'm going to help with the film.

ANATOLY. She's fine. She wants to.

RAISA (*to* IRINA). If you're sure. (*To* ANATOLY.) But look
after her.

ANATOLY. Of course I will.

They go.

Echo Five

*Echoes of Yekaterinberg, as before. The whole Romanov family
are seating themselves on two rows of chairs.*

GUARD. Come on, sit there. We need a picture of you. The
whole family.

ALEXANDRA. Olga's not well, and Alexis –

GUARD. Just do what I say. There we are, the whole nest of
traitors. Traitors to the Revolution.

*We hear the bang and see the flash of old-fashioned photo-
graphic equipment as the family portrait of the Czar and his
children appears on the screen.*

Scene Nine

The next morning, Tuesday 20th August. The big room.

MIKHAIL. How many hours sleep did I get?

RAISA. Not enough.

MIKHAIL. Tuesday the twentieth. Treaty day. The day we were to sign the Treaty that would usher in a new era. Well, I suppose this is a new era.

There is a knock on the door.

Let's see what it brings, eh.

He opens the door. ANATOLY *shepherds in the two little girls in front of him.*

Ah, the new generation.

ANATOLY. What?

MIKHAIL. Sorry, thinking aloud. Good morning.

ANATOLY. Is it?

MIKHAIL. Is it what? Sorry, I'm half asleep.

ANATOLY. We all are, but we thought . . . well, Irina thought . . .

MIKHAIL (*jumping to it*). Yes, of course. Come in, come in.

They do. And the little family ritual begins.

Good morning, Kseniya.

KSENIYA. Good morning, Grandpa.

MIKHAIL. Good morning, Anastasia.

NASTENKA. Good morning, Grandpa.

MIKHAIL. And how did you sleep?

KSENIYA. I didn't.

NASTENKA. I did.

MIKHAIL (*to* NASTENKA). Well, that's something.

ANATOLY. She'd sleep through anything, that one.

MIKHAIL. That's a good sign, Nastenka. It means you have a clear conscience.

NASTENKA. What's that?

MIKHAIL. It means you haven't done anything wrong.

KSENIYA. Have you done anything wrong, Grandpa?

A slight pause, hastily filled by RAISA.

RAISA (*to* ANATOLY). What time did you finish?

ANATOLY. About four. Irina insisted on doing everything with me. She was a great help. She's resting now.

RAISA. Good.

NASTENKA. It's nine o'clock so I don't think she should still be in bed, do you?

MIKHAIL. I think we can make an exception sometimes. It's kind.

KSENIYA. She didn't make an exception. We had to go to bed the same time as always. And I wasn't sleepy.

RAISA. You must try to do what your mother asks.

KSENIYA. Why?

MIKHAIL (*warning*). Kseniya.

KSENIYA. Sorry.

ANATOLY. Come on, we better go back upstairs now.

NASTENKA (*disappointment*). O-oh.

MIKHAIL. Just a minute. Now, what have I got?

He produces chocolate drops.

Now who am I going to give them to?
(*Asking her if she knows.*) Kseniya?

KSENIYA. Nastenka should have them 'cos she's the youngest.

MIKHAIL. Good girl. And Nastenka, what are you going to do
with them?

NASTENKA. Eat them.

ANATOLY *laughs*.

MIKHAIL *shakes his head*.

She corrects herself.

Share them with Kseniya.

MIKHAIL. That's right. And with Mummy and Daddy.

ANATOLY. It's alright, darling, I don't like them.
Come on. (*He gestures to the door with his head.*)

RAISA. It all worked, didn't it, the film?

ANATOLY. Yes, all there. All done. Now all we need is a courier.

MIKHAIL. No hope of that. I can't see it.

ANATOLY. Not for now, but . . .

MIKHAIL. No one can get beyond the terrace.

ANATOLY. Irina said how about one of Oleg's men through
the orchard?

MIKHAIL. Straight into the arms of the perimeter guards? No.
I wouldn't risk it.

ANATOLY. She thought that . . . No, you're right. Well, for now
the tapes are safely stowed. Places Irina found. No one will
get them.

RAISA. Thank God.
She's alright, isn't she, now?

ANATOLY. Yes, I think so.

RAISA. But still let her rest. She's too on edge. Then maybe this afternoon she can come down and we can try and cheer each other up.

ANATOLY. I better get back to listening to the radio.

ANATOLY *goes off with the children.*

Echo Six

Yekaterinberg house. NICHOLAS *is again struggling with the window.*

NICHOLAS. We'll all die in here if I don't get this window open. Olga will suffocate.

ALEXANDRA. Yes. Yes, you're right.

ALEXANDRA *joins in, pushing. Finally the window gives.*

A sigh of relief.

Scene Ten

Tuesday afternoon. On the veranda. IRINA *is nervous and pre-occupied.* RAISA *breathes the air deeply.*

RAISA. Ah! (*Breathes again.*) Free air! This is what I need. Life again.
(*She looks at* IRINA.) Breathe it.

IRINA *takes a breath – less convincingly.*

Better?

IRINA. It's hot.

RAISA. You can smell the peach trees. (*Looks out*.) Look at the sea. It doesn't change whatever they do.

IRINA *is not really looking*.

Just look. Beauty.

IRINA. Soldiers, that's what I see. We're not free.

RAISA. Our hearts can be. Come on, try.

IRINA. How long's this going on?

RAISA. I don't know, Irina, I don't know. But we'll make it. Breathe!

IRINA *tries again*.

IRINA. I shouldn't have left Nastenka down there with the cook. She might eat . . . something poisonous.

RAISA. Old Galina's a true friend. She'll look after her. Anyway, I gave her some of Misha's sweeties.

IRINA. You think of everything.
Kseniya didn't sleep. She cried. Terrible sound. My own child.

RAISA. She's anxious, that's all.

IRINA. I shouldn't have left her. She's not really grown up, whatever she says.

RAISA. Doing the films was important. Tolya told me. You did very well.

IRINA. Did I?

RAISA. Yes.

She touches IRINA*'s arm*.

IRINA. Thank you.

RAISA *turns her attention to the view again*.

RAISA. Just look at that. Blue as far as you can see. When your father and I were young, we used to lie out on the Steppe and look up at that sky and believe it went on for ever. For ever and ever. And we were all part of one great vastness. Then some sharp little ant would come and bite his arm and he'd laugh and sit up . . . and we'd know it wasn't as easy as that.

IRINA. Is he really alright?

RAISA. There are moments when I think he might even cry but then . . . Well, he's just very strong.

IRINA. He passed me on the stairs and didn't even look at me.

RAISA. He thinks of you all the time. He's very worried about you.

IRINA. He needn't be.

RAISA. Good.

IRINA. But I worry about him. I think his blood pressure's up but he won't let me take it.

RAISA. It would only upset him. Just leave it.
(*She looks out again.*) You know, when we first met he still worked on the farm.

IRINA. Yes, the student holidays.

RAISA. Driving a tractor. Sun-burned, hands red raw, but he loved it. His eyes shone more than I've ever seen. Seventeen he was, when he won the Order of the Red Banner – for threshing eight thousand centners of grain with his father. Imagine! Twenty hours a day some days. He says he even fell asleep at the wheel. That award is his proudest honour.

IRINA (*sighing*). Yes.

RAISA. 'Peasant and worker', and he never forgets it. I think a country childhood does you good – look at you. You loved the fields.

IRINA (*flatly*). Did I.

RAISA. Yes. And you were a brave little girl. I'd come home from work feeling guilty I'd left you, and there you'd be, standing on a chair sorting potatoes and stirring the soup.

Just getting on with it. No tears or tantrums. You were a brave little girl.

IRINA. And I'm not now. That's what you mean, isn't it?

RAISA. No.

IRINA. Yes, that's what all this is about. All this 'tractors' and 'farms' and hardiness and 'breathe the air'. It's all 'Be strong! Be brave! Like your father! Like me!' Well, I'm not like you. I'm not. I'm doing my best but I can't do it. I'm not good enough, I know that. I can't keep up with you. I'm letting everybody down, I know I am, I know it.

She breaks down completely.

Oh, help me. Please. Help me, help me. (*She is sobbing desperately.*)

RAISA *hastens to put her arms round her – a passionate, loving embrace.*

RAISA. Oh Irina. Oh my darling. I'm so sorry, I'm so sorry. I didn't mean . . . I thought you were feeling better. Tolya said – I thought –

RAISA *leads* IRINA *inside. Blackout.*

Echo Seven

No longer the Yekaterinberg house.

Now we hear echoes of old fashioned gunfire from Revolutionary days – Czarist troops firing into civilian crowds. Horses neighing, confusion on cobbles, etc.

This cross fades into the much clearer and more immediate crack of modern rifles: Soviet soldiers firing on crowds in Moscow in 1991.

Scene Eleven

Almost as a response to the 'Echo', MIKHAIL is shouting furiously, straight in the face of PLEKHANOV. The big room. It is later in the afternoon of the same day.

MIKHAIL. I demand this be stopped. It must be stopped at once. The troops must be ordered back to barracks. It's monstrous a so-called government is ordering soldiers to fire on our people – turning Moscow into a battlefield. It's like the Czars again.

PLEKHANOV. They judge the situation may get out of control.

MIKHAIL. The situation is out of control. People don't like your coup so they are out on the streets. It's just what I feared.

PLEKHANOV. Or wanted.

MIKHAIL. Feared. It was you who started this, and the only way to restore order is to restore legality and let me out of here and back to my desk in Moscow. It's what the people want.

PLEKHANOV. I'm afraid I can't arrange that.

MIKHAIL. No, you arrange nothing because you are the lackey of a bunch of drunks who have taken over the Kremlin. I don't know that you have even transmitted my demands. But you will transmit this one. The troops will return to their barracks before there is a massacre. We serve the people and you better remember it. They're not yours to kill and maim as you think fit. Now go and tell your masters what the rightful President demands, or you will be responsible for a civil war.

PLEKHANOV *stares*.

Go! Go on!

PLEKHANOV *goes*. MIKHAIL *stands dumbfounded for a few moments then goes out too*.

Scene Twelve

A little later. ANATOLY *standing alone in the big room. It is messy –* RAISA*'s abandoned sewing on the sofa, etc.* RAISA *emerges from the bedroom.*

RAISA. All done. I knew there'd be a place – lining of the curtain. Tiny bit of videotape like that, so light no one will ever notice.

ANATOLY. We thought we'd stowed them all but Irina . . .
Well, I put that one at the back of the toy cupboard and Irina
. . . it's the girls' room, you see, and she thought . . .

RAISA. I can imagine.

ANATOLY. So I had to get it out again.

RAISA. That's fine.
(*Looks at him seriously.*) I don't think you're careful enough with her, you know.

ANATOLY. I'm very careful.

RAISA. She needs to be protected.

ANATOLY. She won't be patronised.

RAISA. I didn't protect her enough as a child. I regret that now.

ANATOLY. 'Protect', 'protect'. You're turning into a mother hen.

RAISA (*startled by this rudeness*). I'm sorry?

ANATOLY. You protect Mikhail too. Protect. It's what you do.

RAISA. I do what is necessary.

ANATOLY. Then talk to him, for God's sake. Tell him what you think – about what's going on with Yeltsin and Moscow. What might be happening. Tell him what I said ten minutes ago. I know you agree.

RAISA. No.

ANATOLY. Confront him. Make him face it. It will do him good.

RAISA. How dare you! How do you know what he thinks or what I say? We've spent our lives discussing politics, he and I, openly, freely, always together. But now working together means me keeping my mouth shut and I will. When I doubt, I hold my tongue, because it's what he needs. He has a thousand worries in his mind and he doesn't need me to poke at them, he doesn't need a doubter at his side. He needs a supporter. So I support.

ANATOLY. And it's killing you.

RAISA. What would you know.

ANATOLY. It is. It must be.

RAISA. OK, it is. But I do my job. And my job now is hopeful, supportive wife. Not easy, but I try. And you, young man, should not be lecturing me.

ANATOLY. No. No. I'm sorry.

RAISA. Well then.

Pause.

ANATOLY. But . . .

RAISA. But what?

ANATOLY. Well . . . Please just think about talking to him. Please. For your sake as well as his. It would do you good.

RAISA *looks at him, almost satirically, but he decides to go on.*

So it's in the open. So you're both prepared, together and separately, for whatever may happen.

RAISA. Really?

ANATOLY. Yes, I think so.

RAISA. So that's your advice?

ANATOLY. Yes.

RAISA. Well, thank you.

ANATOLY. So you will?

RAISA. I said 'thank you', that's all.

ANATOLY. So you won't.

RAISA. Why does it bother you? It's not your business. Anatoly, just go, please, you're upsetting me.

ANATOLY. Yes. Of course. I'll go up to Irina.

He goes. RAISA pauses.

She sits down briefly in the gloomy, fading light. Then she rises and starts restlessly sorting through a drawer, vague and with no real sense of purpose. Suddenly MIKHAIL *enters, snapping on the light.*

RAISA. You've been gone a long time.

MIKHAIL. I went for a walk. In so far as I could get out. I have to use up this energy somehow.

RAISA. Did it do any good?

MIKHAIL. No.
Anyway, I saw him. I told him I demand the soldiers are off the city's streets and returned to barracks.
How's Irina?

RAISA. Oh, she's . . . Tolya will be sitting with her.

MIKHAIL. Have you lost something?

RAISA. I don't know. I was looking for . . . I don't know.

She gestures helplessly at the mess and abandons the drawer.

What did he say?

MIKHAIL. He'll send my orders. That's all.

RAISA. He better.

MIKHAIL. He looked quite shocked.

MIKHAIL *suddenly bursts into song – loudly – a macho Georgian song or maybe a stout song of resistance from the 'Great Patriotic War'.*

RAISA. What are you doing?

MIKHAIL. Singing. Obviously. (*Sings on.*)

RAISA. Must you?

He continues.

Well, at least can't we have something calmer.

MIKHAIL. No.

He continues singing.

She blocks her ears, etc.

I thought you liked my voice.

RAISA. When you serenaded me with ballads, yes. Not this.

MIKHAIL. There's a fire in my belly. I've got to use it.

Sings again. Then breaks off.

What else do you recommend?

RAISA. I don't. I don't. It's alright.

He sings on.

She looks resigned but miserable. So –

He stops. Sighs.

I'm sorry.

MIKHAIL. What then? Perhaps we could sing together?

RAISA. Well . . .

MIKHAIL. Yes, why not. I'll call Irina to play the piano for us. It might do her good.

RAISA. No, let her rest. Please.

MIKHAIL *starts to sing – a gentler song this time.*

MIKHAIL. You know that one?

RAISA. Of course.

MIKHAIL. So . . .

Reluctantly, she joins in. For a while they sing together. She stops and turns away. She can't go on with the charade.

What is it? Raya, what?

RAISA. We can't escape it, can we.

MIKHAIL. Of course not. Not a moment.

RAISA. People are being shot.

MIKHAIL. But resisting. That's hope.

RAISA. Shot.

MIKHAIL. Yes.

Pause.

Raya, I believe that as long as the troops stay calm, this could be a turning point. A turning point, Raya. The soldiers might even change sides. It's not unheard of. In the GDR they didn't even get out of their trucks.

RAISA. That lot wanted to be capitalists.

MIKHAIL. Well, ours don't.

RAISA. We hope.

MIKHAIL. Don't you say that, Raya. Please. Not you.

RAISA. Well, I start to wonder if –

MIKHAIL. Please.

RAISA (*suddenly*). Why can't we just say it! Talk about what we fear.

MIKHAIL. No!

Pause.

RAISA *goes back to her drawer and starts banging about with the junk in it.*

RAISA. Alright. I'm sorry. I'm sorry, I'm sorry. I've been talking to Tolya, that's all. It's what he does to me.

MIKHAIL. I told you, his cynicism is a defence. Hope can be frightening.

RAISA. I know. I'm frightened.
What do you think Yeltsin's up to?

MIKHAIL. Working behind the scenes, I hope. Building up the opposition.

RAISA. You don't believe that. You know that's not his style.

MIKHAIL. Alright, but –

RAISA. He'll be out manning the barricades. Playing the King of Moscow.

MIKHAIL. Maybe.

RAISA. Definitely. Jumping on tanks and making speeches? That was just the start. Now's his big chance.

MIKHAIL. It all helps.

RAISA. Does it?

MIKHAIL. Yes. If he stirs up the people and brings them out on the streets, it's useful. Let him play Saviour of the Nation, I don't care.

RAISA. Saviour of Russia more like. He's not so keen on the rest of it.

MIKHAIL *looks at her hard.*

You know it's true.

MIKHAIL. This is no time for games. He knows that. All that posturing's fine, but not when the whole Union is on the verge of collapse.

RAISA. Maybe that's what he wants.

MIKHAIL (*absolute*). No, Raya, it's not.

RAISA. Alright, not that. Of course not that. Not collapse. But a bit of instability, a few republics breaking away . . . be quite convenient for him, wouldn't it – Russia's rich and manageable, but some of the rest, well . . . ?

He doesn't say anything.

You can't tell me you haven't thought of it. You've been watching him.

MIKHAIL. So he's only backing me because beating the coup will beat the old guard, and after that all the nationalists in the republics can start flexing their muscles? Then get so strong they declare independence? Then the state will break up and Russia will be free to go it alone, and Boris will be King of the Castle and happy? Is that what you think? Is it? And I'll stand by and let it all happen? Is that what you think? Let it!? Well, thank you very much!

RAISA. I didn't say that.

MIKHAIL. Good as.

RAISA. No. But we must talk about it.

MIKHAIL. Why??
    Look, I'm not a fool, Raisa. I'm a politician. I'm not naïve.

RAISA. I know you're not.

MIKHAIL. Well then.

RAISA. But perhaps with people, perhaps . . . when it's people, you . . .
    You're a good man, Misha, so you believe others are good. Maybe you trust too much.

MIKHAIL. Not now.

RAISA. No.

MIKHAIL. Not now. I don't.

RAISA. No, so . . . ?

A tense silence.

MIKHAIL. Boris has his limits. He's not a saint but he's not the devil either.

RAISA (*gives up*). Oh, I don't know.
Things have been going round my head, that's all. I've been sitting here in the gloom and . . . and . . . well, I've only just realised how much I hate him. Boris Nikolaevich is a selfish, dangerous drunk only out for himself. He's as far from you as anyone in the world. And the West will love him.

Pause.

MIKHAIL. We can't choose our allies.
You've never talked like this before.

RAISA. And I don't want to now. But we've got to be prepared for anything. Maybe I'm just letting out all my fears so I can see my hopes more clearly.

MIKHAIL. Well, that's something at least. Don't lose faith, Raya, not now. I couldn't bear it. Shall I tell you my hope? Yes. These are my hopes, Raya, and if you don't share them, I can't go on. I hope . . . I believe . . . that the people's resistance will show how far we've come, that it will be quiet and determined and won't be dispersed by a few guns. They will stand their ground and the soldiers and the plotters will be shamed. And the coup will fail because the conspirators will see that it is no longer 1937, or even '56, and that the people will no longer accept to be subdued by gunfire. Then tomorrow morning, you and I will go back to Moscow and continue to try to give our citizens the country they deserve, where they can breathe and work and talk and think freely, and build a society that is founded on generosity and not on greed. Those are my hopes.

RAISA (*solemn*). Yes. And mine.
(*She breaks into a smile of great affection. With humour, she adds:*) And the Steppe will bloom all the year round.

MIKHAIL (*catching her tone*). And the Steppe will bloom all the year round. Cornflowers and poppies amid the wheat and a cherry blossom for every young girl's hair.

RAISA. So – let's hope for that. I'm happy to hope for all of that.

MIKHAIL. I don't think it's so unrealistic.

RAISA. Because you're a visionary and an idealist and a believer. And without you the world would be a dark place.

Suddenly a volley of shots rings out. RAISA *jumps up.*

Dear God, what's that!?

MIKHAIL. It's Plekhanov's soldiers. He told me they'd fire a practice round at nine – just so we'd know they were there. Not content with killing citizens, now they're ordered to shoot out the stars.

To darkness.

Echo Eight

In blackout. Sound tape – extract from contemporary document – played through speakers as a radio announcement.

RADIO. The doctors appointed by the Committee for the State of Emergency can now report that President Mikhail Gorbachev has suffered a breakdown in the circulation of the blood to the brain. This has left him unable to understand what is going on around him. The President is therefore bedridden and incapacitated. A medical certificate to this effect will soon be made available from doctors on the spot.

Scene Thirteen

*Sudden switch to very bright morning sunlight that bathes the
big room. The door is open and the two children stand lined up
neatly, smiling broadly.* IRINA *stands behind them and it seems
possible this tableau, and the smiles, have been carefully
arranged by her.*

MIKHAIL. Good morning. The new generation greets the day.
With hope. Come in, come in.
How lovely to see you, Irina. (*He kisses her.*) You're feeling
better?

IRINA. Yes.

MIKHAIL. Good. And you're very bright and early. Your
mother's still dressing.

IRINA. I'm sorry, it's just with the sun and everything –

NASTENKA. We wanted to get up.

MIKHAIL. Quite right too. It's only the third morning of our
captivity and regardless of what you hear on the radio, my
mind isn't completely gone yet, so we can't be moping!

IRINA. You sound like Tolya.

MIKHAIL. No bad thing, eh. So –
He's up too?

IRINA. Of course. He'll be here in a moment.

KSENIYA. He can't get up because he didn't go to bed.

MIKHAIL (*to* KSENIYA). Didn't go to bed? Why not?

KSENIYA. Because Mummy made us sleep in her bed with her
and he had to sleep on the floor.

NASTENKA. With a gun.

MIKHAIL *looks at* IRINA *in alarm/questioning.*

IRINA. I thought it would be safest.

MIKHAIL (*far from reassured*). Well.

IRINA. Yes.

MIKHAIL (*turning to the children*). Now come along. Good morning, Kseniya.

KSENIYA. Good morning, Grandpa.

MIKHAIL. Good morning, Anastasia.

NASTENKA. Good morning, Grandpa.

MIKHAIL. I won't ask you how you slept because I think I know.

IRINA. Safely. And sound.

MIKHAIL. Good. Good.

RAISA rushes in from the adjoining bedroom. She is excited, exuberant.

RAISA. Misha, I can see something on the sea.

She catches sight of IRINA *and the children.*

Oh, hello – you're up again!

IRINA. Yes.

RAISA. Good.

She rushes onto the balcony, then with triumphant optimism, exhorts:

Misha, look!

They follow her out.

There. Ships. One, two, three . . . five. Heading toward us. Do you think it's a rescue?

MIKHAIL. They're landing craft.

RAISA. So it could be a rescue!

MIKHAIL. Or –

They are interrupted by an urgent knock on the door.

ANATOLY (*outside the door*). It's me, Tolya.

MIKHAIL. Come in.

He does so.

ANATOLY. Have you seen the sea?

MIKHAIL. Just now.

ANATOLY. It's a blockade, isn't it.

RAISA. Why not a rescue?

ANATOLY. I don't think so.

RAISA. You wouldn't.

MIKHAIL. He's right, Raya. They've cut off the road and the helipad, so why not the sea. Or they're landing more troops.

RAISA. More?

MIKHAIL. It's possible.

IRINA. Oh God.

ANATOLY. I've been listening to the radio.

MIKHAIL. And?

RAISA (*to* IRINA). I think you better take the children upstairs. Can you manage?

IRINA. Yes. Yes. (*To the girls.*) Come on.

RAISA. You'll be alright, won't you?

IRINA *nods.*

ANATOLY. I'll be up in a minute.

RAISA *kisses* IRINA *briefly and she shepherds the girls toward the door.* RAISA *waves to them and they wave back.*

RAISA *and* GIRLS. Bye bye.

IRINA opens the door. At that moment PLEKHANOV *is passing. He stops as he sees them and steps forward into the doorway. Avuncular.*

PLEKHANOV. Ah, the little ones. My Nastenka, good morning. (*He puts his hand out to pat her head.*) How are you –

IRINA (*intervening, nervous/intense*). Leave my children alone. I told you. Please. Please just leave them alone.

PLEKHANOV. I'm sorry, but I . . . I'm only –

IRINA. Leave them!!

PLEKHANOV. Yes, very well.

He withdraws and moves off again.

IRINA waits a few moments on the threshold, looking back tensely at RAISA *and the others.*

IRINA. He's gone.

She and the children leave. The door closes. Pause as they take in her almost hysterical overreaction.

MIKHAIL. Dear God.

ANATOLY. I saw Oleg on the stairs – he said she mustn't let the children out, not even onto the terrace now. They'll be restless but he said he can't guarantee their safety.

MIKHAIL (*sudden outburst*). Can't guarantee their safety! Of course he bloody can't! No one can – we're fucking prisoners! Prisoners! And I'm impotent! The President – no balls. See! I can't even protect my own family.

RAISA. Misha, it's . . . [alright.]

MIKHAIL. But it isn't, is it.

Calming.

He sighs.

Then:

I'm sorry. Sorry.

Composed again.

So. Radio.

ANATOLY. Yes. Well . . . (*He's stalling.*)
I'm afraid there's more news.

MIKHAIL. What? Come on, tell me.

ANATOLY. The BBC says there's another 'delegation' on its way.

MIKHAIL. And . . . ?

More pause.

ANATOLY. It's flying here from Moscow – to confirm, I mean
to check . . . to check on behalf of the people that you are
really incap . . . (*He censors 'incapacitated'.*) Really as ill as
they say you are.

MIKHAIL. Ah.

ANATOLY. Yes.

MIKHAIL. That is, a delegation is flying here to *make* me as ill
as they say I am. That's what you think, isn't it.

ANATOLY. I . . . I don't know.
What do you want me to do?

MIKHAIL. Go back to your room and keep monitoring the
radio. I'll talk to Oleg and make sure our guards are stationed
on all the doors and on the stairs. And the children should be
kept in their room.

RAISA. No, locked.

MIKHAIL. Yes, locked in their room. With some one to look
after them, of course. Galina.

ANATOLY. Yes. Yes. I'll go now.

He does so.

RAISA. Misha, we must hide you.

MIKHAIL. Hide?

RAISA. Yes, we must.

MIKHAIL. I'm not going to hide!

RAISA. But they've come to kill you.

MIKHAIL. We don't know that.

RAISA. If we hide you, it will buy time. We can find out what's going on. They'll be confused, there'll be delay. Maybe we can even escape.

MIKHAIL. We can't escape. I have to face them. What do you want, a lot of men in boots tramping round the house, flinging open cupboards till they finally find the President cowering in the larder, surrounded by fruit and vegetables, staring up from the tiles and begging for mercy? This is me, Raya, I won't do it.

She grabs at him.

RAISA. Please! Please, Misha! For my sake!

Suddenly she clutches her own arm. Is she having a stroke? She goes limp and falls.

Echo Nine

Back in the Yekaterinberg house now. We are in the basement room where the Czar and his family were killed. It is crowded with Romanovs and the gunmen who are to shoot them.

GUARD. Not a photograph this time.

A blast that echoes the earlier photographer's flash, then the terrible shots and ricochets of many bullets firing and bouncing round the confined space. Chaos. The cacophony ends with the dull thuds of the rifle butt that finished off the still whimpering ANASTASIA.

Then silence.

Scene Fourteen

A few hours after Scene Thirteen. MIKHAIL *is alone in the big room.* PLEKHANOV *enters.* MIKHAIL *silently motions him to sit. He does.*

MIKHAIL. Alright, so your hour has come.

PLEKHANOV. What?

MIKHAIL. You heard me. Your men, the ones you work for – your delegation is on its way.

PLEKHANOV. I know.

MIKHAIL. So when they arrive, you better go down and join them.

PLEKHANOV. I intend to.

MIKHAIL. And it'll be your hour of glory. You hope. The day you saved the state. Or lost it. So what exactly will they want?

PLEKHANOV. I don't know.

MIKHAIL. You mean they've kept you in the dark again?

PLEKHANOV. I mean I think it will depend.

MIKHAIL. On how 'incapacitated' I am? That was the word, wasn't it, in the announcement about my health. I'm supposed to be 'incapacitated'.

PLEKHANOV. Are you?

MIKHAIL. You know I am. Have they come to kill me?

PLEKHANOV *looks alarmed.*

Surely that must have crossed your mind – the KGB man who's prepared to take the President prisoner, who countenances soldiers on the streets shooting at civilians.

PLEKHANOV. Look, I'm sorry. I didn't mean to threaten your safety.

MIKHAIL. Only to overthrow the government. I see.

PLEKHANOV. We're not doing that either.

MIKHAIL. Maybe you've changed your minds then. How are things going in Moscow?

No answer.

I know news is rather thin on the ground here, certainly on my side of the house, but I thought you'd be 'up to speed' on that.

PLEKHANOV. Mikhail, this isn't something I've done lightly. I've served you faithfully. I didn't want to see your wife and children held prisoners. I have a family of my own. I understand.

MIKHAIL. You do not.

PLEKHANOV. I do. And I tried to talk to the little ones, to reassure them, but Irina Mikhailovna sent me away. They used to call me Uncle.

MIKHAIL. You really have no idea, do you. My wife collapsed a couple of hours ago. She may have had a stroke. We put her to bed. My daughter's on the verge of a nervous breakdown – no wonder she doesn't want you near her children. My family is strained beyond endurance. This is your doing.

After a chastened pause:

PLEKHANOV. The state is in danger and in the end I serve the state.

MIKHAIL. So do I.

PLEKHANOV. So you know I'm not dishonourable.

MIKHAIL. It depends what kind of state it is. Yours wears jack-boots.

PLEKHANOV. And yours doesn't exist. Can't.

MIKHAIL. It can. My wife says I'm an idealist and a visionary – but I don't think so.

PLEKHANOV. No, you're a liberal, and that's much worse. More dangerous. You'll give the people their head and they'll destroy the country.

MIKHAIL (*very calmly*). Please. Listen to me. This is a turning point, and you're part of it. You can help our nation. Please do. The world has been looking at us and despising us for years – the place where nothing works, where you can't buy a piece of sausage without queuing for an hour, where people are afraid to speak or change anything. The system where even all the rich black earth of the Steppe can hardly produce enough to feed us. Our socialism is failing Yuri, because it is corrupted, stultifying and decayed, and outsiders see it, and they rejoice. We've got to renew – or die. And not just for ourselves, but for the whole world.

PLEKHANOV. The whole world is too far gone.

MIKHAIL. No, they can still hope. We can be their hope. But if our dream fails, our vision of a generous society where people work for each other not only for themselves, not just to beat their neighbour or because they fear to die in a ditch, but for the good . . . if we lose that, we'll have destroyed one of the most noble aspirations of mankind.
WE CAN'T – AFFORD – TO FAIL.

PLEKHANOV. Mikhail, you've failed already.

MIKHAIL. No, don't you see! Don't you *seeee*! (*He is almost tearful*.) We must keep on going, we must keep trying. We can make it work. All of us together.

PLEKHANOV. This is nonsense.

MIKHAIL. It's the soul of our state! What it was made for.

Pause.

Help me. Join with me. Your last chance. Tell those men from Moscow that they owe it to the people to be true social-ists, not Stalinist oppressors. Order the soldiers they've put in your command to take no part in the coup. It will be a noble act, symbolic and powerful.

PLEKHANOV. And wrong. You've untied the string and it's our job to bind it up again. The senior people are all against you. Even old Marshall Yazov's with us.

MIKHAIL (*saddened*). Yazov?

PLEKHANOV. Yes. Even he knows where you're going.

MIKHAIL. You don't trust the people, that's your trouble. The lot of you.

PLEKHANOV. It's Western advertising we don't trust, consumerism, pornography . . . all that tide of vicious, contagious, corrupting greed! The way technology's going, soon we won't be able to stop it, so we must protect the people, protect them – before the filth swamps them.

MIKHAIL. Our people want a just society.

PLEKHANOV. They want big cars and designer clothes.

MIKHAIL. They'll never forget their brother. Ever.

PLEKHANOV *looks away – embarrassment? disgust? or shame perhaps? Then:*

PLEKHANOV. Have you really not learned, Mikhail? Really?

No response.

That virtue must be policed.

MIKHAIL. So you're a Stalinist now.

PLEKHANOV. No.

MIKHAIL. Yes. Reverting to type. We're the same age, both of us have grandfathers who were taken away. Innocent men sent to prison camps. Remember it.

PLEKHANOV. I do.

MIKHAIL. But you're KGB – that's the difference, isn't it, between us. It always comes back to that. The heart. When I was younger, just about forty, the new President befriended me – Andropov, he'd just been installed – and he and I, we'd

share our holidays. I remember one night we sat out under
the stars, a bonfire blazing, and he looked up, and talked of
all his hopes and dreams for our country – so noble, so
inspiring – and I thought that he could change the world. But
when it came to it, he did almost nothing. Didn't try. Fifteen
years Chairman of the KGB – it had cramped his heart. He
could never be more than a servant of the system. An appa-
ratchik. That's all he was. And a suspicious man too, in the
end. Like you.

Pause.

PLEKHANOV. When the delegation arrive they will demand to
see you.

MIKHAIL. I won't meet them.

PLEKHANOV. They will require it.

MIKHAIL. Well, I have my requirements too. And they must be
complied with before I'll see them.

PLEKHANOV. It's not going to be like that.

MIKHAIL. You mean you'll use your soldiers to force the
matter?

PLEKHANOV. No, I don't think so.

MIKHAIL. What then? I shall order my guards to take the delegation into custody.

PLEKHANOV. They won't find that possible.

MIKHAIL. I shall order it all the same.

PLEKHANOV. Alright, so you'll make the gesture.

MIKHAIL. But not seeing them won't be a gesture. And if
your soldiers come like thugs with guns and drag me into
their presence, I shall refuse to speak. My brain and tongue
can't be coerced, whatever else you can control.
Free will – I have it.
My demands are these, you've heard them before: the full
restoration of all communications, including government

communications, and a plane back to Moscow. That's it. I have nothing to negotiate. Their alternative will be to shoot me. In the meantime, I will attend to my wife.

PLEKHANOV *shifts in his seat and looks as though he might rise, but he doesn't – he's transfixed by* MIKHAIL *who is looking straight at him.*

You've shrunk, Yuri Sergeyevich. You're less than you were. Drawn back inside like a shrivelled nut.

PLEKHANOV *doesn't respond.*

It's the death of the soul.

PLEKHANOV *rises to go.*

Where do you think you're going? I haven't dismissed you yet.

PLEKHANOV (*his retaliatory ace*). Haven't you forgotten who's in charge now.

He goes.

MIKHAIL *takes some moments to recover from this interview. Perhaps he just sits there or maybe wanders to the window.*

After the shock, he's thinking hard.

With new resolution, he is just on the point of setting off to the bedroom to see RAISA *when there is a little scrabbling sound at the door and she enters – rather frail and tottery.*

RAISA. It's only me. Are they here yet?

MIKHAIL. No, no.

He hastens to help her.

RAISA. Irina said it would be alright to get up, if I was careful.

As he sits her along the sofa with her feet up and spreads the rug she is clutching over her:

MIKHAIL. Are you sure?

RAISA. Yes, yes. I couldn't not be with you, the strain would be worse.

MIKHAIL. How are you feeling?

RAISA. It wasn't a stroke. She's positive. She's given me some blood-pressure pills and says I must rest. Not the time for it really, is it. Then I'll be fine.

MIKHAIL. Fine?

RAISA. Well, you know.
I think it's good for her – having to be professional.

MIKHAIL. What it is to have a doctor for a daughter. More use than a president for a husband.

RAISA. I married a great man. I don't regret it.

Silence.

I thought I heard shots when I fell.

MIKHAIL. There were no shots.

RAISA. Like the Czar's family – Yekaterinberg. You know. Maybe I was dreaming.

MIKHAIL. You were, my darling.

RAISA. But it frightened me. It was like this for them, wasn't it. A house in the middle of nowhere, the whole family held prisoner . . . then shot.

MIKHAIL. We won't be shot.

RAISA. No.

MIKHAIL. And we're not the Czar. We're *saving* the Revolution. Saving it. And they won't take it from us.

RAISA. No.

MIKHAIL (*firmly*). No. I think they're coming out of weakness not of strength.

RAISA *looks questioning.*

I think –

They are interrupted by a door knock. ANATOLY *identifies himself and enters.*

ANATOLY. They've arrived.

MIKHAIL. How many? Who?

ANATOLY. Two cars full. Lukyanov and Kryuchkov in the first one.

MIKHAIL (*takes it in*). Well now.
Lukyanov, Raya. So there's another traitor for me. We were students together – remember him then?

RAISA. Yellow hair. Your friend. Oh Misha.

ANATOLY. Plekhanov's troops all lined up to salute them when they came in. Your guards could do nothing.

MIKHAIL. I was expecting that.

ANATOLY. I felt sick.
And they've taken over the ground floor like they own it.

MIKHAIL *notes this. Then:*

MIKHAIL. I've told Plekhanov I won't see them. Not till they restore all my communications.

ANATOLY. Is that wise?

MIKHAIL. Essential. Make them sweat.
I have my reasons. Trust me.

ANATOLY. I do, Misha, but . . .

MIKHAIL. Trust me.

ANATOLY. So we're just to wait?

MIKHAIL *nods.*

I'll go and tell Irina. She's much better, you know.
(*Modifying.*) Well . . .

RAISA. Yes she is.

MIKHAIL. Good.

ANATOLY goes.

I'll try to be calm but I won't be.

RAISA. What are you doing? You won't do anything reckless.

MIKHAIL. I never do.

RAISA. No, but . . . Alright.
But what if they just lose their patience and storm in and . . .

MIKHAIL. I don't believe they will. Please, Raya, let's just
wait. Till I'm proved right.

RAISA (*after a pause, decisive and matter of fact*). Could you
bring me my sewing then? I think I shall do some sewing.
Got to get that dress finished for Nastenka.

MIKHAIL. I married the right woman. Courage in adversity.

RAISA (*mock brightness*). What adversity? Sewing please.

He brings her the peasant dress. She begins to sort threads, etc.

They are startled by an abrupt knock on the door.
PLEKHANOV *announces himself loudly from outside and*
marches straight in without waiting to be asked.

PLEKHANOV. The delegation has asked me to inform you
that restoring communications as requested will take too
long. They cannot accept the delay. They demand to see
you at once.

MIKHAIL. I decline. My requirements remain. Tell them.

PLEKHANOV. They won't like it.

MIKHAIL. Too bad.

PLEKHANOV goes.

RAISA. They're in a hurry, Misha. Why are they in such a hurry?

MIKHAIL. In a country where it still takes two months to get a
new wheel for a tractor, I can't think. It's intended to intimi-
date me. It doesn't.

RAISA. Nor me.

She starts sewing again with as much determination as she can muster.

MIKHAIL *crosses to a table with bottles on it, selects vodka and pours.*

MIKHAIL. I am a Russian, after all. (*He drinks.*) Want some?

RAISA. Yes please.

MIKHAIL. Will it go with your pills?

RAISA. Who cares.

He hands her a glass.

MIKHAIL. Better than chocolate drops. I should have thought of it before, but I generally leave the drinking to Boris. And of course my esteemed Deputy. I bet the Vice President, sorry, the Acting *President* is practically under his desk by now.

RAISA. Let's hope.

MIKHAIL (*toasting*). 'To the Russian people, Glasnost, Perestroika, and the renewal of true Socialism.'

MIKHAIL *downs his drink in the traditional Russian fashion. So does* RAISA.

Another?

RAISA. No, one's enough.

MIKHAIL. I will. There's too much adrenalin for it to have much effect.
(*Pours for himself. Toasting.*) 'Damnation to our enemies!'
(*Drinks.*) The sons of dogs, of pigs, of swine, of polecats, hyenas, of . . .

His litany is interrupted by a knock on the door. ANATOLY *identifies himself and enters with* IRINA. *She is very upright and on a very tight rein.*

IRINA. I hope you don't mind, but we couldn't stay up there.

MIKHAIL. Of course not. It's right that we should all be together. Help yourself to vodka if you like.

IRINA does. ANATOLY at first signals 'no', then changes his mind. Downs it in one. IRINA clutches her glass and sips cautiously.

IRINA. I want to bring the children down but Tolya says I can't.

MIKHAIL. He's right. They're much safer where they are.

ANATOLY. No one will even know they're there. That's the point.

Another fierce knock at the door. Another abrupt entrance.

PLEKHANOV. It can't be done. They must see you at once. They insist.

MIKHAIL. Do they.

PLEKHANOV. Yes.

MIKHAIL. Well, I insist too, so what do they propose to do about it?

PLEKHANOV. Well, they . . . (*At a loss.*)

MIKHAIL. Yes?

PLEKHANOV. They are very senior people, the Chairman of the Supreme Soviet, the Chairman of the KGB, the –

MIKHAIL (*interrupting*). Precisely.

PLEKHANOV. So they . . . I know you're the President but you must realise that they –

MIKHAIL (*interrupting*). Oh, I do realise.

PLEKHANOV. So you must see them.

MIKHAIL. Tell me, are they carrying pistols? Or knives?

PLEKHANOV looks puzzled.

Or cleavers? Or bludgeons? Or rope? Or maybe they plan to torture me with burning brands – Comrade Lukyanov on one side and Comrade Kryuchkov on the other – then if I won't agree to their demands, chain me up by the heels and hack off my head with an axe.

PLEKHANOV. Of course they d – [don't.]

MIKHAIL. – Of course not. Exactly. So go and tell them I insist. I will not meet them until they have restored full communications. And then – we'll see.

PLEKHANOV *goes*. ANATOLY *looks questioningly at* MIKHAIL.

My last throw. He's on the run, see. Did you see the look on his face?

ANATOLY. He did look a bit . . .

MIKHAIL. 'Non-plussed' – yes, that would be the word. I like that. A word for someone bewildered, caught in the middle, in doubt. A rabbit in the headlights. Well, he can stay there. And when he decides to run, let's hope he doesn't go the wrong way.

ANATOLY. I know you're the stronger.

MIKHAIL. I am. He said I was a liberal, but I can be absolute when I need.

RAISA. Be careful, Misha.

MIKHAIL. I have all the cards. They expect me to crumble. I shan't.
Listen, all of you. I believe – I believe we are nearly home. The Chairman of the Supreme Soviet? The head of the KGB? You don't send men like that to murder a president.

ANATOLY. No.

MIKHAIL. No, you do it at a distance, with a long arm, quietly. Then deny it.

ANATOLY. Or disown it.

MIKHAIL. Precisely. So the Czar was murdered by regional troops, 'out-of-control local extremists without orders', so they said, and Moscow could do nothing about it. That was the story. But this time, they've sent the big-wigs. Moscow itself has come to Mahomet. Anything that happens will be undeniable.

So we are safe, Raya, and the longer we keep them waiting, the better.

RAISA. But surely they . . . mightn't they just lose their tempers and order the soldiers to come in and –

MIKHAIL. No, because they're cautious men. Our bureaucracy doesn't breed Napoleons, you know. They're cautious and they're worried and they've come to find a way out. The longer we leave them, the more they'll worry – worry about the people massing on the streets, worry about what they're going to do about them . . . They think they may have let things go too far already and they're getting scared. They're scared of the people! Isn't that wonderful! Scared of the people – that's our achievement. We've given them the space to think for themselves and unless they're shot by the hundred like Tiananmen Square, they'll back me. And no one, not even the plotters, wants a Tiananmen Square. So they'll climb down. Them, the plotters. Not me. Not the people.

ANATOLY. That's pretty convincing.

MIKHAIL. I believe it.

ANATOLY. So do I.

MIKHAIL. Do you? Anatoly the realist?

ANATOLY. Yes.

IRINA. I believe it too.

MIKHAIL. So we wait, and call their bluff. Like poker.

The wait begins in earnest. ANATOLY *and* IRINA *gravitate together.* MIKHAIL *tries to sit by* RAISA *but he's very fidgety.*

What do sensible people do?

RAISA. Do?

MIKHAIL. While they wait? They don't talk about it, do they. They talk about something else. The weather. Hot. Not much else to say there, is there. Sport? Well . . . (*Despairs of finding a chat line.*) I'm sorry, I'm making it worse. I'll go away.

RAISA. No, no.

She holds out her hand to him as he moves off. Then she resumes her sewing but soon abandons it.

ANATOLY *and* IRINA *go and sit by her.* MIKHAIL *remains alone.*

Restlessly, he lifts the telephone but it is still dead.

A pack of cards catches his eye and he picks it up.

He takes it down to a little table and starts to try to build a house of cards.

The light is on him: his hands are shaking and it's not easy. It takes time – perhaps the lighting suggests more time than literally passes – but eventually he gets a good house up and growing.

But his hand knocks it and it collapses.

MIKHAIL. I should stick to chess. More Russian.

He gets up and goes and lifts the phone again. Still dead.

He returns to behind RAISA *as she sits on the sofa. He puts his arms on her shoulders and bends to put his cheek on hers.*

Then moves off again.

Eventually, he arrives back at the phone. He lifts it again.

Eureka!

It works! It works! I don't believe it. We've done it! We've done it!

He seems about to cry. ANATOLY *and* IRINA *run to hug him.* RAISA *attempts to rise but she is frail.* MIKHAIL *makes his way to her side with the other two still clinging to him. Eventually they are all together in one joint embrace. Tearful.*

They've given in. We're saved. We've saved hope.

Cue music, lights, fireworks, Georgian champagne corks, the lot!

The children rush in to join. Wild celebration, Russian style.

After a while, we realise MIKHAIL *has moved to one side. In a separate, quiet space created by light, he lifts the phone and dials. He speaks:*

(*Into phone.*) Boris – it's me. (*Listens.*)

Yes, I'm alive. We all are. And the phones are back on. They've given in. (*Listens.*)

I know you have. And they never would have done it without you. You and the people. So thank you. (*Listens.*)

I thought so. Thank you. You've been magnificent. (*Listens, then calls over to* RAISA.) They're sending a plane from Moscow to get us.

(*Into phone.*) Thank you. I can't thank you enough.

With MIKHAIL *still holding the phone, the celebration scene disappears and transforms into . . .*

Scene Fifteen

Everyone still on stage, now including PLEKHANOV. *Ideally the dacha, etc. has vanished – it's a bare stage.* MIKHAIL *slowly replaces the phone's receiver. He's thoughtful, in a world of his own and remains separated from the others – perhaps seated.* KSENIYA *and* NASTENKA *are now sitting on the floor surrounded by toys and gadgets with which they are pre-occupied. Among other things,* KSENIYA *plays on a laptop and* NASTENKA *studies some girls' magazines. Sometimes the adults speak out front.*

MIKHAIL. The first person I rang was Boris Nikolaevich Yeltsin.

PLEKHANOV. That was a mistake for a start.

MIKHAIL. He was . . . he . . . he sounded very relieved. He'd been very brave.

PLEKHANOV *gives him a contemptuous stare.*

I should have rung my mother. I know that, but somehow I couldn't. I regret it.

RAISA. You rang her the next day from Moscow.

PLEKHANOV. But first, you rang Yeltsin.

ANATOLY. August the twenty-first, 1991: the day of our liberation.

RAISA (*to* MIKHAIL). I've never seen you look so grey as during those three days imprisonment. I watched you every moment, my darling. I could almost see you changing. So drawn, so tense, so exhausted.

MIKHAIL (*to* RAISA). You looked exhausted too.

RAISA. I was. Near the edge.

IRINA. So was I.

ANATOLY (*to* IRINA). You were like a zombie at the end.
When we put you on the plane . . . Your little blue skirt . . .
your eyes so wide and glassy.

RAISA. It was the not saying, the avoidance. I longed to talk to
you openly but . . .
It made me very . . .

MIKHAIL. I know.

ANATOLY. August the twenty-first, 1991: the day of our
liberation.
We returned to Moscow and the streets were full of people.
They were shouting . . .

PLEKHANOV. Oh yes, they were shouting.

RAISA. They were shouting . . .

PLEKHANOV (*to* MIKHAIL). Not for you. Not for 'Gorby'.

IRINA (*in sorrow, to* MIKHAIL). Not for you. Not for the
returning hero.

PLEKHANOV. But for Yeltsin. Boris Yeltsin. He was their
saviour. Boris, the one who yelled from the top of the tank,
Boris, the one who waved his arms and promised Freedom –
while you were stuck in a dacha dreaming of socialism.
(*With heavy sarcasm*.) What nobility you showed, eh?
Then on August the *twenty-third*, 1991, two days later . . .

ANATOLY. He, Boris Yeltsin, the new hero, ordered the Soviet
Communist Party to suspend activities in the Russian
Republic.

IRINA (*to* MIKHAIL). The Party you'd worked for all your
life. The Party . . .
Oh Daddy.

PLEKHANOV. It was in the Russian parliament. (*To*
MIKHAIL.) You were there. You had made a speech to thank
him, Comrade Yeltsin.

ANATOLY. Thank him.

PLEKHANOV. Then he produced a paper, a decree.

ANATOLY. Suspending the party.

PLEKHANOV. He got out his pen and raised it – ready to sign. You tried to intervene.

MIKHAIL (*re-enacting*). 'Stop! I . . . I . . . '

ANATOLY. But you have no power.

PLEKHANOV (*mimes signing, then, as Yeltsin*). 'There it is. Signed.' And it was. And the Deputies applauded.

MIKHAIL *looks away.*

IRINA. Applauded.

PLEKHANOV. And the Russian national flag was hoisted over the Kremlin, and Yeltsin began secret manoeuvres to undermine the unity of the USSR. 'Gorbachev must be kept out of the game,' he said.

IRINA. Out.

ANATOLY. So much for your ally.

PLEKHANOV. Boris Yeltsin comes from Sverdlovsk, you know that, don't you? Sverdlovsk – called Yekaterinberg in the Czar's time. Yekaterinberg: Sverdlovsk. Sverdlovsk: Yekaterinberg. The same place brings in the beginning and the end. Ironic, that. You like ironies, don't you, Mikhail?

MIKHAIL *looks away.*

Something to do with your subtle mind.

ANATOLY. September the twenty-second, a month after the attempted coup – Estonia, Latvia, Belorus, Moldavia, Georgia, Azerbaijan, Kyrgystan, Uzbekistan, Tajikistan, Armenia, and the Ukraine had all declared independence from the Soviet Union.

PLEKHANOV. So much for your Treaty!

MIKHAIL. We hoped . . .

RAISA. We hoped –

PLEKHANOV. Ah yes, 'Hope'! And your faith in the people. Well, at least you had me arrested. That must have been some satisfaction.
But then on the first of January, 1992 . . .

Maybe RAISA *crosses to* MIKHAIL *here.*

On the first of January, 1992, you had to agree that the USSR would cease to exist, Russia would be an independent state . . .

ANATOLY. Boris Yeltsin would sit in your desk in the Kremlin . . .

RAISA. . . . and you would resign.

Pause.

MIKHAIL. Yes.
'I resign.'

PLEKHANOV (*to* IRINA). Not a god, then.

IRINA. No, not a god.

RAISA. But a good man.

IRINA (*to* MIKHAIL). But I thought you could save . . . I thought . . .

PLEKHANOV. No.

MIKHAIL. No.

ANATOLY. No. Reality.
'The suicide of the Soviet Union,' that's what someone called it.

RAISA. 'It's like another fall of man,' my mother would have said.

PLEKHANOV. The great experiment, over. In less than seventy-five years.

MIKHAIL (*de profundis*). You blame me. I know it.

PLEKHANOV. Yes.

MIKHAIL. I . . . (*Near breaking point.*)

PLEKHANOV. Yes.
> All the things I told you would happen, happened – swept away on a tide of greed and chaos and misery. Oligarchs, and beggars dying in the snow.

ANATOLY. Clutching bottles of vodka.

RAISA. Fake vodka.

ANATOLY. And no state to help them.

PLEKHANOV. But at least they were free! Oh yes, free! – free to starve, to chase goods most of them could never hope to get and to live in a broken country with a third of its land and most of its power gone. Was that your vision?
Was it?
Was it!?
Because that's what you led to, what you let your 'people' choose. Yes, I blame you – because left to themselves, people are greedy fools.

MIKHAIL. No.

PLEKHANOV. No?

MIKHAIL. No. I'll never lose faith in the people.

RAISA (*echoing him*). . . . never lose faith in people.

> PLEKHANOV *is not impressed.*

> *A moment.*

> When I was a little girl, there were Germans in our village. POWs. The war was nearly over and they were prisoners, but they were still Germans and we'd heard all about them. All the stories. Germans were evil men, racists, murderers, stupid savages, people who needed good leaders to curb them. And these were Hitler's days, and leaders were very, very bad. So these Germans, these POWs, we knew them. We knew what they were like – and we were scared.

It was an autumn day, a cold wind, birch leaves blowing by,
and my sister and I were out playing – when one of these
POWs stopped in front of our house. Big coat, black boots,
scrubby face. Dark. Huge. Oh, he looked the part. Then he
tried to talk to my little sister. She was only six. I hung back.
I just watched. I was scared. Then slowly, horribly slowly, he
put his hand out to touch her. His hand! Her hair! I rushed
forward and grabbed her and she clung to me. I put my arms
round her to protect her and we were terrified. Terrified! Of
this brutal man. This *person*, this German.
Then I looked up at him. He had half turned his head away
from me, shielding it, he put one hand to his eyes. But I
could see . . . I could see his face . . . and I could see, I could
see . . . that he was young.
And he was crying.

Pause.

PLEKHANOV. What's all that supposed to mean?

RAISA. If you don't know . . .

IRINA. Don't you know?

Pause.

PLEKHANOV. I remember I put my hand out once, to her
(*Indicates* IRINA.) little girl . . . And she . . . I . . . (*He is
unwilling or unable to go on.*)

IRINA. Yes, I remember.
And I'm sorry now.

ANATOLY (*to* PLEKHANOV). So you do know what it means.

PLEKHANOV. Yes.

MIKHAIL. Yes.
And you know that . . .

His attention and ours has been drawn to the children:

Little NASTENKA *is now busily applying make-up and
admiring herself in a hand-mirror.*

KSENIYA *is at her laptop and is playing a suddenly very noisy and obviously violent computer game.*

Attracted by it, NASTENKA *goes to her and tries to snatch the control from her hand.* KSENIYA *fights her off.*

(*After watching the girls.*) . . . that even with all that –

ANATOLY. – for the haves. What about the others?

MIKHAIL. Even with all that –

RAISA. – there's still hope.

PLEKHANOV. Are you sure?

The End.

A Nick Hern Book

The President's Holiday first published in Great Britain in 2008 as a paperback original by Nick Hern Books Limited, 14 Larden Road, London W3 7ST in association with Hampstead Theatre, London, and the Nuffield Theatre, Southampton

Cover image: www.n9design.com
Cover design: Ned Hoste, 2H

Typeset by Nick Hern Books, London
Printed and bound in Great Britain by Biddles, King's Lynn

A CIP catalogue record for this book is available from the British Library

ISBN 978 1 85459 575 1